Companion to
Emma

Patrick Murray

THE EDUCATIONAL COMPANY OF IRELAND

First published 1990
This reprint 1994

The Educational Company of Ireland Limited
Ballymount Road
Walkinstown
Dublin 12

A trading unit of Smurfit Services Limited

© Patrick Murray

Cover photograph courtesy of BBC Television

Proofreading: Clodagh Brook

Disk conversion and Layout: Phototype-Set Ltd.

Printed in the Republic of Ireland by
Citiprint Ltd., Dublin

123456789

Contents

The Structure of *Emma* and Some Key Chapters • **5**

Society in *Emma* • **29**

Some Themes of the Novel • **49**

Irony in *Emma* • **61**

The Characters of the Novel • **69**

For Discussion • **103**

The Structure of Emma

(A) GENERAL COMMENTS

JANE AUSTEN'S use of Emma as the focus of almost everything that happens gives the novel a unified structure. As F.R. Leavis pointed out, 'Everything is presented through Emma's dramatised consciousness'.

The action of *Emma* moves in clearly-defined parts like the acts of a play. There are three related movements in the novel, with Emma as the focus of each. As one movement gives way to the next, Emma's positive influence over what happens diminishes. There is also a beautifully-worked out double action. As events develop, Emma's social importance diminishes, as she is gradually obliged to recognise her proper place in the overall scheme of things. But her loss of social dominance is paralleled by her moral growth. The three main movements of the novel are as follows:

The first movement (Chapters 1 to 15) is a comedy of self-deceit, the main theme of which is Emma's determination to bring about marriage for Harriet Smith (with Mr Elton) or to prevent it (with Robert Martin). This movement ends in the scene in the carriage where Mr Elton proposes to Emma, making it clear that he considers Harriet a social inferior, which is how Emma considers him. The result of Emma's complicated intrigues on behalf of Harriet is humiliation for herself at being proposed to by Mr Elton, and a feeling of guilt at having encouraged Harriet to like a man who has no interest in her.

The second movement (Chapters 16 to 46) is dominated by Emma's relationships with Elton and his new wife Augusta, and also with Frank Churchill, whose love-affair with Jane Fairfax is one of many shocks with which Emma is confronted.

Emma's dealings with Frank Churchill are complicated. It does not take her long to develop the illusion that Churchill is in love with her, a notion presented with exquisite irony in Chapter 26 ('Emma divined what every body present must be thinking. She was his object, and every body must perceive it'). She surrenders her illusion when, becoming bored with Churchill, she projects him as a suitable match for Harriet, still pursuing vigorously her hobby of match-making and her ambition to manage the lives of others. The complicated relationships involving relatively few central characters in *Emma* are neatly underlined in Chapter 32, where Elton is in the same room at once with the woman he has just married (Augusta), the woman he had wanted to marry (Emma) and the woman whom he had been expected to marry (Harriet).

This second movement marks a perceptible decline in Emma's importance. Knightley observes this when he remarks: 'Your neighbourhood is increasing and you mix more with it'; this increasing neighbourhood absorbs and diminishes Emma. Two indications of this are her threatened exclusion from the dinner party given by the Coles, and Frank Churchill's readiness to manipulate her for his own purposes. There was a time when Emma would have been the manipulator.

The third movement (Chapter 47 to the end) confronts Emma with her most considerable shock so far. In Chapter 47, the pivotal chapter of the novel, she has to reap the unfortunate harvest of her match-making activities and her interference in the lives of others, particularly in relation to Harriet Smith. Emma has long encouraged Harriet to think herself entitled to marry a man of social distinction. The man Harriet has finally chosen is, unfortunately for Emma, her own friend and close confidant, Mr Knightley. Harriet's revelation that Knightley is her choice has one vital result: it makes Emma 'acquainted with her own heart', forces her to confront the essential truth about her attitude to Knightley ('It darted through her, with the speed of an arrow, that Mr Knightley must marry no one but herself!').

Vital transitions in the novel, and in Emma's development as a character who must gradually learn the truth about herself and others, tend to involve scenes between herself and Knightley. In these scenes, Knightley usually makes her aware of her shortcomings and errors of judgement. Four of these scenes are especially important. The first is in Chapter 8, where Knightley reproves Emma for persuading Harriet to reject Robert Martin, as her inferior in social standing. Mr Knightley's verdict on this is uncompromising: 'A degradation to illegitimacy and ignorance, to be married to a respectable, intelligent gentleman-farmer'. Knightley explains to Emma that her intimacy with Harriet is very foolish, likely to influence Harriet to despise her equals and to seek to marry above her social station. At this point, Knightley's sound advice has little or no influence on Emma. She is entirely convinced that her opinions on Harriet are right and Knightley's wrong, and is 'absolutely satisfied with herself'.

The second scene in which Knightley tries to influence Emma's attitude to another character is in Chapter 18. Here the subject is Frank Churchill. Knightley knows only that Churchill is 'well-grown and good-looking, with smooth, plausible manners', but instinctively reaches the reasonably accurate conclusion that the young man, whom Emma is determined to admire, 'may have learnt to be above his connections, and to care very little for anything but his own pleasure'. For all this, Emma remains prejudiced in Churchill's favour; again Knightley's strong, sensible views have no real effect on her attitude.

The third scene in which Knightley gives Emma the benefit of his solid wisdom is in Chapter 33. Here the character under discussion is Jane Fairfax. This time there is a much closer affinity between Knightley's views and Emma's. Knightley believes that Jane lacks 'the open temper which a man would wish for in a wife', while Emma rejoices to hear that Jane has a fault.

There is a fourth occasion on which Knightley takes on the role of Emma's moral tutor and advisor on conduct and attitude. This is in Chapter 43, which has a crucial place in the moral scheme of the novel. In this chapter, Mr Knightley takes Emma severely to task for her cruelty to Miss Bates. This time,

Knightley's words have a deep influence on Emma's thinking about herself: she at last arrives at an awareness of her defects. She feels anger against herself, mortification, deep concern. She feels tears running down her cheeks. This scene marks a significant alteration in Emma. She is thoroughly chastened and mortified. She is rightly convinced that her altered self can now meet Knightley's highest demands: 'Could he even have seen into her heart, he would not, on this occasion, have found anything to reprove'.

(B) SOME KEY CHAPTERS IN *EMMA*

Chapter 4

THE central theme of this chapter is Harriet Smith's attachment to Robert Martin and Emma's subtle and effective attempts to undermine this attachment, first of all by discrediting Robert in various ways and then by proposing a new object for Harriet's admiration: the vicar Elton. Among Emma's methods of undermining Harriet's interest in Robert Martin are the following suggestions:

(a) that his mental horizons are limited by farming and that he does not read;

(b) that such a yeoman farmer must necessarily be below Emma's own notice;

(c) that Martin, being only twenty-four, should not marry until he is thirty. Emma knows that a delay of this kind will discourage Harriet;

(d) that Harriet, Emma fancifully suggests, is a gentleman's daughter, and so should marry somebody who will maintain her as a lady;

(e) that Martin's 'remarkably plain' appearance is com-

pounded by his 'entire want of gentility';
(f) that there is a world of difference between Martin and real gentlemen like Mr Knightley, Mr Weston and Mr Elton.

The rival candidate for Harriet's affections, envisaged by Emma, is Mr Elton. In Elton's favour are the following factors:
(a) His manners are superior even to Mr Knightley's. He is cheerful, obliging and gentle.
(b) He might be recommended as a model for any young man.
(c) He has warmly praised Harriet to Emma.

The importance of this chapter lies in the fact that it contains the genesis of Emma's misguided scheme to pair off Elton with Harriet, a scheme which will have such troublesome and embarrassing consequences for Emma when Elton proposes marriage to her in Chapter 15.

The ironies in Chapter 4 are largely at Emma's expense. She is unaware of the problems she is creating for herself and others by interfering in Harriet's life. Her most confident declarations ('There can be no doubt of your being a gentleman's daughter') turn out to be sadly ill-founded (Harriet is the daughter of a tradesman).

There is also some fine irony in Emma's account of Elton's virtues. As she sees him here, Elton is quite the gentleman 'without low connections'. In Chapter 16 she will take a much less flattering view of his social position and background ('the Eltons were nobody'; Elton is 'without any alliances but in trade').

Chapter 8

SOME important issues arise in this chapter. The most interesting aspect of the chapter is its presentation of the Emma-Knightley relationship. These two central characters of the novel are free spirits, lively, intelligent and argumentative. At this point in the novel, the older and wiser Mr Knightley tends to be the more dominant of the two. This dominance is suggested in Emma's reflection that 'she did not always feel so absolutely satisfied with herself, so entirely convinced that her opinions were right and her adversary's wrong, as Mr Knightley'.

In this chapter, at any rate, Mr Knightley's opinions are much more sensible than Emma's. The main topic of discussion between them is the future of Harriet Smith. Mr Knightley is anxious to see Harriet marry a sensible young farmer, Robert Martin, while Emma believes that such a match would be beneath the dignity of her young friend. Mr Knightley has advised Martin to propose to Harriet; Emma has persuaded Harriet to reject the proposal. This leads to an animated debate between Emma and Mr Knightley.

The central point of difference between the two concerns Harriet. Mr Knightley has a low opinion of her ('the foolish girl ... she is not a sensible girl, nor a girl of any information ....'). He believes that marriage to her would involve a degradation for Martin, not for Harriet. When Emma suggests that Robert Martin is Harriet's inferior as to rank and society, his reply is crushing: 'A degradation to illegitimacy and ignorance, to be married to a respectable, intelligent gentleman-farmer!' Mr Knightley recognises that Robert Martin is Harriet's superior both in rank and situation. Emma, unlike Mr Knightley, does not like facing unwelcome facts and prefers fantasies ('There can scarcely be a doubt that her father is a gentleman').

Knightley's role as Emma's mentor and moral guide is clear in this chapter. He does all he can to guide her ideas and actions along sound lines. He points out, for example, that Emma's intimacy with Harriet is a very foolish one from Harriet's point of view. Emma, he rightly divines, will fill Harriet with exaggerated notions of her own importance, with ideas beyond her station. The result will be contempt for men of her own class. ('She knows now what gentlemen are; and nothing but a gentleman in education and manner has any chance with Harriet'). This is Emma speaking, and she is pleased with the sentiment. Knightley knows something at this stage that Emma will have to learn quite painfully and to her cost. Elton is the man Emma has in mind for Harriet. Knightley knows enough about Elton and about human nature to recognise the folly of proposing a match between Harriet and Elton. As he tells Emma, 'Elton may talk sentimentally, but he will act rationally'. Elton's reason, as Mr Knightley predicts, leads him to marry an heiress.

The chapter features one of Jane Austen's finest ironies. Referring to Harriet, Emma says to Mr Knightley: 'Were you, yourself, ever to marry, she is the very woman for you.' The irony of this is completed towards the end of the novel when Emma is tormented by the possibility that Mr Knightley may indeed marry Harriet.

Chapter 15

THE early part of this chapter is given over to two concerns which frequently disturb the peace of mind of characters in Jane Austen's novels: minor illnesses and weather. Illness, and the risk of contracting it, dominates much of Mr Woodhouse's thinking; his obsession is the subject of gentle irony (he is 'awake to the terror of a bad sore throat'). He is terrified lest Emma pick up Harriet's throat infection, 'more anxious that she should escape the infection than that there should be no infection in the complaint'. Inclement weather is another cause of alarm, even panic. Mr Weston knows that snow has been falling, and is reluctant to mention this fact for fear of alarming Mr Woodhouse. Isabella's alarm at the snowfall is equal to her father's, although the snow turns out to be no more than half an inch deep.

The climax of the chapter, and one of the central episodes in the novel, is Elton's declaration of his love for Emma. We are subtly prepared for Emma's negative response when we are told that even under ideal circumstances, Elton's company was not utterly desirable to her; if she could have talked of Harriet, 'the three-quarters of a mile would have seemed but one'. There is irony in the ignited Elton's proposal to Emma; the lover she has been proposing for Harriet now professes himself her lover. Furthermore, it transpires that Elton does not realise that he has been Harriet's lover at all! He has never cared whether Harriet lived or died but as Emma's friend; if Harriet 'has fancied otherwise, her own wishes have misled her'. The irony here is that it is not really Harriet, but Emma, who has 'fancied otherwise'.

We learn much about Elton in this chapter. He is, as Mr Knightley rightly divines, a fortune-hunter. He also has contempt for any kind of alliance that will not advance his own social status ('I need not so totally despair of an equal alliance, as to be addressing myself to Miss Smith').

The encounter with Elton and the indignity of his proposal mark a major turning-point for Emma, who now realises the folly of her relationship with Harriet.

Chapter 16

EMMA'S experience with Mr Elton has led to a useful growth in her self-awareness. She has been self-assured, supremely confident in her own judgements of people. She now realises how much better a judge of character Mr Knightley has been. There is much irony in Emma's reflections on Elton. Earlier she has found him 'good humoured, cheerful, obliging and gentle'; now, following his mistake of proposing to her instead of Harriet, she thinks him 'proud, assuring, conceited; very full of his own claims, and little concerned about the feelings of others'. All Elton has done to deserve this totally new and unfavourable opinion is to propose to her. This offends her high sense of her own importance: Elton has no right to consider himself her equal in connection or in mind. Elton has also struck a blow against her policy of manipulating others and bending their lives to her wishes. Her criticism of his conduct to her and to Harriet has strong elements of comedy as well as irony:

> But — that he should talk of encouragement, should consider her as aware of his views, accepting his attentions, meaning (in short), to marry him! — should suppose himself her equal in connection or mind! — look down upon her friend, so well understanding the gradations of rank below him, and so blind to what rose above, as to fancy himself showing no presumption in addressing her! — It was most provoking.

Emma's blindness to the real implications of what she is thinking here is the source of the irony of this passage. She does not realise that if Elton has been unreasonable in wanting to marry above himself on the social scale, Harriet would be equally unreasonable in wanting to do so, and she herself unreasonable in encouraging her. It is a case of Emma wanting to have things both ways.

Elton's proposal has also affected her rational views on his character and background. Earlier on, she has found him gentleman-like and well-connected, a model for other young men, superior in one respect even to Mr Knightley. Now that he has proposed to her, however, she regards him as a fortune-hunter, only wanting to 'aggrandise and enrich himself'. She now also decides that the family from which he comes 'were nobody', and that he himself is 'without any alliances but in trade', and without anything to recommend him to notice but his 'situation and his civility'. In such ways, Jane Austen makes her heroine the victim of subtle irony.

Emma, who has made an occupation of match-making, now realises that it was foolish and wrong of her to take an active part in bringing any two people together. As future events will show, she has not quite learned her lesson in this regard. In Chapter 31, we find her speculating on the possibility that Frank Churchill may be in love with Harriet ('he had been very much struck with the loveliness of her face and the warm simplicity of her manner').

 **Chapter 20**

THIS chapter belongs to Jane Fairfax. Since she is destined to marry Frank Churchill, it is interesting to note that Jane Austen draws a parallel between the upbringing of these two young people. Frank Churchill and Jane both live with adoptive families, and keep relatively little contact with their real ones.

Although the chapter deals with Jane, its main source of interest is Emma's attitude to her. This attitude is subtly presented and analysed. Emma is not particularly attracted by the prospect of Jane's arrival; she is sorry to have to be civil to a person she does not like 'through three long months'. Why Emma should dislike Jane is not at all clear. The two ought to be natural friends and companions. Mr Knightley's explanation is probably the most plausible: Emma sees in Jane the accomplished young woman she wants to be thought herself. There is also the problem that Jane has been made such a fuss of by everybody.

Like all the other characters, Jane serves to throw light on Emma's mental processes and attitudes. Some of these reflect an astonishing naiveté and an over-developed imagination. The latter is, of course, her main problem. Without any kind of evidence, she has spun a web of intrigue and deception around Jane Fairfax, Mr Dixon and his wife. Jane Austen allows us to contemplate Emma's attitudes ironically. Emma, resolved to dislike Jane no longer, is now 'willing to acquit her of having seduced Mr Dixon's affections from his wife'. However, she still contemplates 'the highly probable circumstance' of an attachment on Jane's part to Mr Dixon. This kind of fantasy is typical of Emma's thinking throughout the novel. Having abandoned one fantasy, she still harbours another: that Jane has done the decent thing and given up her hopes of Mr Dixon! This notion enables Emma to form a higher opinion of Jane than she has previously had ('nothing could be more pitiable or more honourable than the sacrifice she had resolved on').

Emma has resolved to give up match-making following her lesson from Mr Elton. She is, however, still incapable of breaking her old habit entirely. Her instinct to arrange the lives of others now comes to the surface. She leaves Jane with 'softened, charitable feelings', and begins to lament that 'Highbury offered no young man worthy of giving her independence, nobody that she could wish to scheme about for her'.

This chapter shows how volatile Emma's feelings are. Her charitable feelings for Jane do not last very long. Soon, she sees Jane as being 'disgustingly' and 'suspiciously' reserved, and returns to her fantasies about Jane and Mr Dixon.

Emma's imagination blinds her to the real truth about Jane: that she is involved with Frank Churchill. As her mind hovers around the relationship between Jane and Frank Churchill, she becomes annoyed that her curiosity about the nature of this relationship is not being satisfied. Jane politely declines to give her any solid information about Frank, and Emma cannot forgive her.

All in all, the chapter shows the extent of Emma's need to control the affairs of those around her, her tendency to interfere, and her considerable curiosity.

Chapter 26

THE long-awaited arrival of Frank Churchill has added a new interest to Emma's life. Her imagination, which has already played her false with Mr Elton and Harriet, now begins to work on Frank Churchill. The latter and Emma are among the guests of the Coles in this chapter. Later we are to discover that Frank Churchill is secretly engaged to Jane Fairfax before his arrival at Highbury. Throughout this chapter, Emma is thinking and acting in ignorance of this, and is therefore the victim of irony. Frank is anxious to ensure that his engagement remains a secret. In an effort to disguise it from public knowledge, he is prepared to let it be thought that he is interested in anybody else except Jane. Emma misinterprets Frank's behaviour towards herself as a clear sign of romantic interest; her overactive imagination supplies the supposed evidence for this. Here is how she interprets Frank Churchill's sitting beside her:

> The son (Frank) approached her with a cheerful eagerness which marked her as his peculiar object, and at dinner she found him seated by her — and, as she firmly believed, not without some dexterity on his side.

This is not the end of Emma's flood of speculation. Frank Churchill makes straight for the place where Emma is sitting, and will not sit until he can find a seat near her. Jane Austen presents Emma's reaction with splendid irony: 'Emma divined what every body present must be thinking. She was his object, and every body must perceive it'. Emma's imagination is again to the fore when the subject of Jane's new piano is raised. Again, Emma thinks of every explanation except the real one, which is that the piano is a present from Frank Churchill. She is perfectly convinced that Mr Dixon is the source of the present, which she sees as 'an offering of love'.

The most significant aspect of the chapter is Emma's response to the possibility that Mr Knightley may marry. A hint of the hidden strength of these feelings is provided in her response when Mrs Weston thinks of a match between Jane and Mr Knightley:

> 'Mr Knightley must not marry! You would not have little Henry cut off from Donwell? Oh! no, no. Henry must have Donwell. I cannot at all consent to Mr Knightley's marrying; and I am sure it is not at all likely. I am amazed that you should think of such a thing.'

Little Henry is Emma's nephew, the son of Mr Knightley's

brother John. If Mr Knightley does not marry, Henry will inherit his property. We will find out later that Emma's concern for little Henry does not go very deep: when she herself decides to marry Mr Knightley, Henry's claims are easily forgotten.

The chapter has some fine comic touches. Emma's lively imagination conjures up a delightfully incongruous vision of Mr Knightley, married to Jane Fairfax, having to endure Miss Bates 'belonging to him', and thanking him for marrying Jane.

Emma is a novel of multiple ironies. In Chapter 26 we have a subtle example. Mrs Weston takes on some of Emma's imaginative qualities and her role as match-maker as she conjures up a marriage between Mr Knightley and Jane, with Emma in the uncharacteristic role of advocate of common sense and reason.

Chapter 32

IN this chapter we are introduced to Mrs Elton, one of Jane Austen's supreme comic creations. The arrival of this lady on the scene brings a new liveliness and verve to the novel. With Mrs Elton present, there is never a dull moment.

It is interesting to notice that Emma's view of Mrs Elton is more accurate than her views of most of the other characters. She finds 'ease but not elegance' in Mrs Elton, and in this her judgement is sound. Her comments to Harriet on the subject show the abrasive side of Emma's character. When, for example, Harriet expresses no surprise that Elton should have fallen in love with Augusta, Emma offers this riposte:

> 'Oh, no, there is nothing to surprise one at all — A pretty fortune, and she came in his way.'

And again,

> 'Miss Hawkins perhaps wanted a home, and thought this the best offer she is likely to have.'

Mrs Elton's social deficiencies emerge in this chapter, and are exposed to merciless scrutiny. The result is some brilliant social comedy. Mrs Elton is a clearly individualised character, but her social mannerisms are universal; we have all have met people who exemplify some or all of her more disagreeable modes of behaviour. Everybody has met the kind of person who likes to boast of well-placed relatives ('My brother Mr Suckling's seat') and of the petty details of their domestic arrangements ('The laurels at Maple Grove are in the same profusion as here').

Mrs Elton is best seen as a modified version of both Mrs Bates and Emma. Like Mrs Bates, she has a vacuous mind which finds a ready outlet in idle chatter. Her conversational range is limited to a few ideas, the repetition of which is a source of amusement ('and that will be our time for exploring ... we shall explore a great deal, I dare say ... They will have their barouche-landau, of course ... we should be able to explore the different beauties extremely well ... I shall decidedly recommend their bringing the barouche-landau ... Mr Suckling is extremely fond of exploring ... We explored to King's Weston twice last summer, in that way, most delightfully, just after their first having the barouche-landau'). The iteration of 'exploring' and 'barouche-landau' renders this passage increasingly ludicrous. Like Emma, Mrs Elton likes to arrange the lives of others. When she offers to manage Emma's own social arrangements, the latter is indignant; this is as fine a piece of irony as any in the novel, since Emma herself is constantly engaged in arranging the lives of others.

Another feature of Mrs Elton's character illustrated in this chapter is her extreme egotism. She believes that everybody is fascinated by the smallest details of her life, and that she has an enviable command of her destiny ('Blessed with so many resources within myself, the world was not necessary to me'). She is capable of shocking social lapses ('I must do my *caro sposo* the justice to say that he need not be ashamed of his friend. Knightley is quite the gentleman'). Little wonder that Emma finds her 'a little upstart, vulgar being'.

 **Chapter 33**

THIS chapter, like Chapter 32, is dominated by Mrs Elton. Her role is that of a foil to Emma; she also functions as a vulgar parody of Emma as arranger of the affairs of other people. Just as Emma has taken up Harriet Smith and tried to dictate the course of her emotional life, so too Mrs Elton now wants to 'assist and befriend' Jane Fairfax. The relationship between Mrs Elton and Jane is a reminder of Emma's earlier enthusiasm for Harriet. Mrs Elton's motives in patronising Jane are fundamentally egotistical. She thinks her public interest in the young woman will reflect credit and glory on herself. The subject of helping Jane gives her an opportunity to boast ('My acquaintance is so very extensive, that I have little doubt of hearing of something to suit her shortly').

The chapter features various types of conflict. Emma and Mrs Elton see each other as natural enemies. From Mrs Elton's point of view, a state of warfare with Emma makes it natural for her to patronise Emma's rival, Jane Fairfax.

As in every chapter of *Emma,* we find here a rich vein of irony. It is ironic, for example, that Emma, who has neglected Jane Fairfax, her natural companion, should criticise Mrs Elton for patronising her. As in the previous chapter, Emma's thoughts are here the subject of ironic contemplation. She is still seen as harbouring fantasies about Jane and Mr Dixon:

> 'Poor Jane Fairfax!' thought Emma, 'You have not deserved this. You may have done wrong with regard to Mr Dixon, but this is a punishment beyond what you can have merited — the kindness and protection of Mrs Elton!'

The chapter offers some subtle insights into Emma's thoughts not only on Mrs Elton, but on Mr Knightley. As in Chapter 26, she is still not conscious of the true depth of her feelings for Mr Knightley. One thing is clear, however: she does not want him to marry Jane, and the possibility that 'little Henry', her nephew, may be disinherited is still her official reason for being alarmed at the possibility that Mr Knightley may marry.

Chapter 38

THIS is one of the central chapters of the novel, and it brings many issues to a head. In earlier chapters, we are given hints of Emma's interest in Mr Knightley. This chapter takes the process somewhat further. Up to now, we are made to feel that Emma's attitude to her friend and mentor is a negative one: he must not marry anybody else. In this chapter, we see why he is the only man *she* can marry. He is the only one who can command her unqualified admiration. Her reflections on him are frank and more explicitly flattering than before:

> His tall, firm, upright figure, among the bulky forms and stooping shoulders of the elderly men, was such as Emma felt must draw everybody's eyes, and excepting her own partner, there was not one among the whole row of young men who could be compared with him.

Jane Austen often achieves a great deal through the use of an apparently insignificant incident. This incident is used to shed important light on the Eltons and Mr Knightley. Mr Elton is ready to dance with Mrs Weston when the latter asks him to dance with Harriet Smith. His response is a source of deep embarrassment to Harriet ('Anything else I should be most happy to do at your command — but my dancing days are over'). It is at this point that Mr Knightley reveals his true moral worth. To Emma's delight, he rescues Harriet from her mortification by dancing with her. The Eltons are thoroughly discredited by this incident. They celebrate Harriet's discomfiture with 'smiles of high glee' and sarcasm ('Knightley has taken pity on poor little Miss Smith').

The sequel to this incident is an interesting piece of dialogue between Emma and Mr Knightley. The key portion of this dialogue, from Emma's point of view, is Mr Knightley's assessment of Harriet Smith. He allows that she has 'some first-rate qualities, which Mrs Elton is totally without. An unpretending, single-minded artless girl — infinitely to be preferred by any man of sense and taste to such a woman as Mrs Elton. I found Harriet more conversable than I expected.'

The comment on Emma's attitude (she 'was extremely gratified') has ironic overtones. Very soon, she will be in an agony of suspense and doubt over Harriet's relationship with Mr Knightley and will be far from 'gratified'. The events at the Ball, however, will help to bring to a head her own relationship with Mr Knightley, and force her to acknowledge the depth of her feelings for him.

Chapter 43

THE chapter begins happily for Emma. Frank Churchill does all he can to amuse her, to be agreeable to her, and to flatter her. Mrs Elton finds Frank's attentions to Emma thoroughly disagreeable and will write letters to her friends telling them that 'Mr Frank Churchill and Miss Woodhouse flirted together excessively'. Frank's language to Emma certainly supports this point of view ('You order me, whether you speak or not. And you can be always with me. You are always with me').

The reaction of the Eltons to the attention being given to Emma by Frank and to her presiding role in the Box Hill entertainment makes them comic figures. Mrs Elton, who likes to preside over everything, grows angry when Frank places Emma at the centre of things. A game is organised in which

Emma is to hear what everybody is thinking of; Mrs Elton gracelessly refuses to enter into the spirit of anything she herself has not arranged ('It is a sort of thing which I should not have thought myself privileged to inquire into').

Mrs Elton's social lapses show her ill-mannered boorishness, but now Emma betrays a remarkable degree of insensitivity. A new game is organised, in which the participants are required to say one very clever thing, two moderately clever things, or three very dull things. Here is the crucial piece of dialogue. Miss Bates begins:

> 'I shall be sure to say three dull things as soon as ever I open my mouth, shan't I? .... Do you not all think I shall?'

Emma could not resist.

> 'Ah! ma'am, but there may be a difficulty. Pardon me — but you will be limited as to number — only three at once.'

This is easily Emma's worst moment in the novel. Nothing that Mrs Elton says is anything like as offensive. Mr Knightley is appalled, and tries to make her conscious of the gravity of her lapse ('How could you be so unfeeling to Miss Bates? How could you be so insolent in your wit to a woman of her character, age and situation?').

To give Emma her due, she responds with a proper sense of shame to Mr Knightley's exposure of her wrongdoing. She feels anger against herself, 'mortification and deep concern'. Her suffering is emphasised again and again ('Never had she felt so agitated, mortified, grieved at any circumstance in her life').

Meanwhile, the Eltons go their own sour, humourless way, doing their best to spoil whatever enjoyment the others may be having. They are left to their own devices.

 **Chapter 44**

M R KNIGHTLEY'S rebukes have stirred Emma's conscience, and she is now determined to make amends to Miss Bates for her insensitive remarks. She observes that Miss Bates is less at ease in her company than she used to be, but a kind enquiry after Jane Fairfax restores the old feelings.

Jane refuses to see anybody and Miss Bates is forced to resort to a white lie ('I am afraid Jane is not well'). At this point we are given a glimpse of the new Emma, a softer, gentler person than before. As the novel approaches its climax, Emma's character undergoes some profound but subtly-rendered changes. She has already felt sorrow and mortification over her attempt to involve Harriet with Elton. She now begins to entertain benevolent feelings towards Jane, knowing that the latter has problems ('and this picture of her present sufferings acted as a cure of every former ungenerous suspicion, and left her nothing but pity').

Emma's pity seems well deserved. Jane is due to become a victim of Mrs Elton's patronage, and to become a governess, the occupation she hates most, and regards as the equivalent of slavery. Her strong feelings on the subject are made clear in Chapter 35. Places where governesses are hired are 'offices for sale — not quite of human flesh — but of human intellect'. Miss Bates's account of Jane's destiny is brilliantly rendered by Jane Austen. The account shows how much Miss Bates's thinking has been conditioned by Mrs Elton. The speaker is Miss Bates, but it might as well be Mrs Elton. The effect is pathetic and comic at the same time:

> 'To a Mrs Smallridge — a charming woman — most superior — to have the charge of her three little girls — delightful children. Impossible that any situation could be more replete with comfort; if we except, perhaps, Mrs Suckling's own family, and

Mrs Bragge's; but Mrs Smallridge is intimate with both, and in the very same neighbourhood: — lives only four miles from Maple Grove. Jane will be only four miles from Maple Grove'.

This, and the rest of what Miss Bates has to say, is an amusing parody of Mrs Elton's discourse throughout the section of the novel in which she enforces her ideas and personality on everybody around her. Miss Bates, not having much of a mind of her own, parrots Mrs Elton's chatter about Maple Grove and the little Sucklings and the little Bragges. She also believes in Utopias in which governesses are paid huge salaries and lead lives of pleasure. Emma's realistic view of the 'governess trade' is the necessary corrective to these fantasies:

> 'Ah! madam', cried Emma, 'if other children are at all like what I remember to have been myself, I should think five times the amount of what I have ever yet heard named as a salary on such occasions, dearly earned.'

Fortunately for Jane, she will not have to be a governess after all, thanks to developments announced in the next two chapters.

Chapter 47

THIS is one of the finest chapters in the novel, and brings to a head all of Emma's proceedings in relation to Harriet. It is the chapter in which Emma is forced to confront the consequences of her interference in the lives of others. This interference now threatens to blight her own prospects of happiness.

The chapter is fraught with irony and is rich in the comedy of misunderstanding. Emma, as usual, is the victim of most of this misunderstanding and of the irony arising from it.

The chapter opens with Emma full of sympathy for Harriet who, as she imagines, will be devastated when she hears that Frank Churchill is engaged to Jane Fairfax. This is only one of Emma's miscalculations in the chapter. As it turns out, Harriet is not in the least disturbed by the news of Frank Churchill's engagement, and is able to reassure Emma ('You do not think I care about Mr Frank Churchill'). In the circumstances, there is delightful irony in Harriet's compliment to Emma ('You .... who can see into everybody's heart ...'). As it happens, Emma cannot see into anybody's heart, certainly not Harriet's, as we are soon to discover. The following piece of dialogue represents one of the major turning-points of the novel. Harriet has been expressing amazement that Emma should have believed her in love with Frank Churchill, and declaring her attachment to somebody 'infinitely superior' to everybody else:

> 'Harriet!' cried Emma, collecting herself resolutely — 'Let us understand each other now, without the possibility of further mistake. Are you speaking of Mr Knightley?'
> 'To be sure I am. I never could have an idea of anybody else — and I thought you knew. When we talked about him, it was as clear as possible'.

It was certainly not clear to Emma. The source of the misunderstanding is identified. Harriet never once named Mr Knightley as the man of her dreams, and seemed to Emma to be referring to Frank Churchill. The following passage provides the key to the misunderstanding:

> 'Oh! Miss Woodhouse, believe me! I have not the presumption to suppose — Indeed! I am not so mad — But it is a pleasure to me to admire him at a distance — and to think of his infinite superiority to all the rest of the world, with the gratitude, wonder and veneration, which are so proper, in me especially'.
> 'I am not at all surprised at you, Harriet. The service he has rendered you was enough to warm your heart'.

> 'Service! oh! it was such an inexpressible obligation! The very recollection of it, and all that I felt at the time — when I saw him coming — his noble look — and my wretchedness before ... From perfect misery to perfect happiness.' (Chapter 40)

Emma thinks Harriet is referring to Frank Churchill's rescue of her from gipsies; she is really referring to Mr Knightley's dancing with her at the Crown Inn. The exchanges between Harriet and Emma on the subject of Mr Knightley are shot through with irony. Harriet is now another Emma, letting her imagination take over from reality. The irony is that it is Emma who has encouraged her to entertain unreal hopes, and who must now endure the possibility of seeing Mr Knightley marry Harriet. It is this possibility that proves decisive for Emma, as we learn from two of the key sentences of the novel:

> A few minutes were sufficient for making her acquainted with her own heart ... It darted through her with the speed of an arrow that Mr Knightley must marry no one but herself.

Other important truths flood into Emma's mind under the impact of Harriet's revelation. She knows now that her conduct towards Harriet all along has been unfortunate, amounting to 'blindness' and 'madness'. The full consequences of her influence on Harriet become apparent when the latter gives her present view of Robert Martin ('I hope I know better now, than to care for Mr Martin, or to be suspected of it'). Emma has encouraged Harriet to be upwardly mobile socially, and not to be content with the relatively humble Robert Martin. She has learned the lesson all too well, and is content only with the most eligible man in the neighbourhood, Mr Knightley, and even feels his equal ('But now I seem to feel that I may deserve him, and that if he does choose me, it will not be anything so very wonderful').

Emma has at last acquired the kind of self-knowledge she has lacked from the beginning. She has been living 'entirely under a delusion', and 'totally ignorant of her own heart'. The following passage, which is an interior monologue, conveys the extent of Emma's growth in insight and self-awareness:

> With insufferable vanity had she believed herself in the secret of everybody's feelings, with unpardonable arrogance proposed to arrange everybody's destiny. She was proved to have been universally mistaken ... she had done mischief. She had brought evil on Harriet, on herself; and, she too much feared, on Mr Knightley.

What troubles her most, apart from her fear that she will lose Mr Knightley, is that he will debase himself by marrying Harriet, 'be captivated by very inferior powers'. The great ironic question comes towards the end: 'Who had been at pains to give Harriet notions of self-consequence but herself?'

Chapter 49

THE happy outcome to the relationship between Emma and Mr Knightley is the subject of Chapter 49. This outcome is not, however, brought about without some suspense. Both Emma and Mr Knightley are obliged to remain a while in doubt about each other's feelings.

At the beginning of the chapter, Mr Knightley thinks that Emma must be suffering on account of Frank's engagement to Jane Fairfax. Here we have a parallel with the situation in Chapter 47, when Emma thought that Harriet must be in need of consolation at the very same news. It takes Emma some time to make Mr Knightley realise that she is not particularly concerned over Frank's engagement; he feels it necessary to assure her at first that 'time will heal the wound'. Then comes her firm declaration of her own attitude to Frank Churchill and her explanation of the latter's mysterious conduct:

> 'It was his object to blind all about him; and no one, I am sure, could be more effectively blinded than myself — except that I was not blinded — that it was my good fortune — that, in short, I was somehow or other safe from him.'

Frank Churchill blinded all about him to his interest in Jane because he knew that if this interest became known to Mrs Churchill she would raise violent objections. Mr Knightley now knows that Emma had no real interest in Frank Churchill, but wonders whether she may accept him as a husband. He envies Frank Churchill, he tells Emma, in one respect. This leads to some confusion on her part:

> 'You will not ask me what is the point of envy — You are determined, I see, to have no curiosity — You are wise — but I cannot be wise, Emma. I must tell you what you will not ask, though I may wish it unsaid the next moment.'
> 'Oh! then, don't speak it, don't speak it', she eagerly cried. 'Take a little time, consider, do not commit yourself.'

Emma thinks that Mr Knightley is about to seek her advice on the subject of Harriet, and she wants to avoid that topic. Soon Mr Knightley makes her realise that Harriet is nothing to him, and she herself everything. He has been in love with her, and jealous because of Frank Churchill. The chapter ends with Mr Knightley and Emma in a state of perfect happiness.

Society in *Emma*

(A) GENERAL OBSERVATIONS

A CLASS-RIDDEN SOCIETY

SOCIETY in *Emma* is a carefully-structured affair. There is a strong consciousness of class differences and distinctions, most people knowing their own place in the social scale and acting accordingly. Generally speaking it can be said that the novel upholds a conservative social outlook. It is true that Emma has to learn to deserve her social position by treating those somewhat inferior to her socially, like Miss Bates, with respect and consideration, but her social position is never called into question. We know almost from the start that the lowly-born Harriet Smith will not cross the rigid social boundaries which mark off the various classes from each other by marrying either Mr Knightley or Frank Churchill.

Emma is mortified when Mr Elton proposes to her: in the world of Highbury, a marriage between Mr Elton, who has not fully arrived, socially, and a great heiress like Emma would not be proper. Certainly this is how Emma sees it. She is as insulted by his hopes of marrying her as he is by the notion that he should marry Harriet ('the natural daughter of somebody'). She sees it as a major fault in Elton that he wants to breach the established social boundaries:

> He wanted to marry well, and having the arrogance to raise his eyes to her, pretended to be in love .... He only wanted to aggrandize and enrich himself; and if Miss Woodhouse of Hartfield, the heiress of thirty thousand pounds, were not quite so easily obtained as he fancied, he would soon try for Miss somebody else with twenty, or with ten.

The novel is filled with indications that there are superior people and inferior people, and that the latter ought to preserve an attitude of proper deference towards the former. Emma is able to contemplate the marriage of her sister Isabella to John Knightley with pleasure because the latter belongs to 'a family of such true gentility, untainted in blood and understanding'. Isabella has connected herself to a family whose members are never likely to depart from the highest social standards, having 'neither men, nor names, nor places, that could raise a blush'. It is clear that Emma's attitude here has Jane Austen's approval and that the reader is also expected to approve of it.

Again, the vital importance of recognising the claims of rank and social class is enlarged on at length after Elton has committed the unforgivable blunder of proposing marriage to Emma, his social superior. Emma overstates the case, but we are expected to give a qualified approval to what she has to say about the true order of society. How, she wonders, could Elton suppose himself her equal in connection or mind? How could he be so conscious of 'the gradations of rank below him', by spurning Harriet Smith, and so blind 'to what rose above' him by presuming to propose to Emma?

The importance of birth, breeding, pedigree, source of income, occupation and reputation in establishing one's social position is memorably conveyed by Emma in her reflections on the social gulf that is fixed, at least in her mind, between her own family and that of Mr Elton. For one thing, the Woodhouses have been settled for several generations at Hartfield, the younger branch of a very ancient family, while the Eltons 'were nobody'. More significantly, the Woodhouses are great landed proprietors with a large fortune, while Elton is a mere *parvenu,* having entered the neighbourhood only two years ago, obliged to make his way in the world 'without any alliances but in trade' and with nothing to recommend him but his position as a parson and his civil manner. The social distinction between a great landowning family and one merely connected with trade is the vital one here.

THE ROLE OF MONEY

The role of money in Highbury society is a complex one. Much of Emma's social superiority derives from the fact that she is worth thirty thousand pounds. In the world of Emma, if two people are to marry, it is most desirable that there be an equality of income. This explains the strong views of Mrs Weston, not a particularly mercenary person, on the engagement of the rich Frank Churchill to the penniless Jane Fairfax. Because of the huge disparity of fortune between the two, Mrs Weston decides that 'it isn't a connection to gratify'.

The case of the Coles offers an interesting insight into the significance of money as a lubricant to social esteem and acceptability. The Coles are decent, friendly, unpretentious people but from the point of view of genteel society, they labour under some major disabilities. The are 'of low origin, in trade, and only moderately genteel'. In recent times, however, they have begun to enjoy a considerable increase in income, and are able to afford dinner-parties. Emma ponders the new situation of the Coles. She supposes that they will hardly presume to invite 'the regular and best' families in the neighbourhood to these parties. They might now be considered respectable in their own way, but in Emma's view, 'it was not for them to arrange the terms on which the superior families would visit them'. Finally, the superior Emma condescends to visit the Coles, whom she and her father have ignored for social reasons for ten years. Newly acquired money has made the difference.

It is important to recognise that by no means everybody of consequence in Hartfield takes Emma's attitude to questions of social importance. Social attitudes in the area may be conservative, but they are not as irrevocably fixed and static as Emma's are. For instance, she persuades herself that she can have nothing to do with the farming class to which Robert Martin belongs. If Harriet Smith marries Robert Martin, then as Emma sees it, she will be confined to a social circle that superior people, including Emma, will have no desire to enter. But we must remember that Emma's closest friends, Mr Knightley and the Westons, have acquaintances of all classes at Highbury. We are made to feel that Emma's greatest single weakness is her arrogant isolation from the world around her. Part of her cure is that loneliness tempts her to mix more in the social life of Highbury. She does not, for example, relish the thought of being left in 'solitary grandeur' while all her neighbours are being entertained by the Coles. When we first meet Emma she is preoccupied with those things that divide each social rank from those immediately above and below it. Towards the end, she has a somewhat more liberal and informal attitude to rank and social status.

A careful reading of the novel will reveal the dynamic quality of Highbury society. Over a few generations many families have risen from 'respectability' to the possession of 'gentility and property'. The characters in *Emma* are mainly the 'genteel' people of Highbury. There are subtle social differences between these. One index of gentility is whether the person in question is considered suitable for an invitation to the Woodhouse home. Some genteel families are, and some are not. Miss Bates and her mother, who have dwindled from prosperity to poverty, are often invited to Hartfield, while wealthier families, newly enriched, are not. Consider, too, the contrast in social terms between Mr Weston and Mr Cole. The former, originally an officer in the militia, then successful in trade, has made a fortune and climbed higher in the social scale than the latter, who has not yet managed to overcome his inferior origins despite his commercial success. Genteel people over whom there hangs no question mark include John Knightley and Mr Perry. Knightley is a successful lawyer who has married Emma's sister, while Perry is an 'intelligent, gentleman-like man'. It is also considered safe to invite Elton the vicar.

(B) THE LIMITATIONS OF JANE AUSTEN'S SURVEY OF SOCIETY

AN UNDEMOCRATIC SOCIETY

JANE AUSTEN was a member of the genteel bourgeois class, and this is reflected in the social outlook of her novels. She was not interested in social reform; she believed that most of the class distinctions she depicts in *Emma* were right and proper. The standards she reflects would not, and could not, apply at large in a modern democratic society where people like Emma and Knightley would have to work for their living as Robert Martin does. We cannot blame Jane Austen if her world appears at odds with our own; we must accept her rendering of the society she knew, understood and valued. This, however, cannot prevent us from looking at the novel in the light of our own social experiences.

What Jane Austen took for granted as right and inevitable was an aristocratic, structured view of society in which inequality of the most extreme kind was absolutely inevitable. A hostile commentator might say, with some justice, that the values and standards of Emma's world are founded on the belief that it is right that a small minority in the Highbury community should enjoy a prosperous way of life at the expense of an impoverished majority. Jane Austen nowhere brings this notion to the surface of *Emma*. For her, the interesting social distinctions are not between prosperous, genteel people and the very poor, but between various kinds of genteel people.

The very poor do not appear as individual characters, since Jane Austen confines herself to the kinds of people she understands: the middle and upper-middle classes in an English village. In this restriction, she is generally allowed to have acted wisely. It saved her from embarrassing condescension towards servants and working-people on the one hand, and unsureness in the face of aristocrats on the other. Many critics praise her for writing about what she understood, and avoiding what she did not. There can be few readers of Jane Austen who would willingly surrender the novel she actually wrote for fiction of social protest or reform, or a document exposing the cruel lot of labourers and tenants.

THE LIVES OF THE POOR

Jane Austen does not entirely exclude the deprived social classes from consideration: she devotes part of a chapter to a revealing coming together of two divided and distinguished worlds, as Emma, accompanied by Harriet Smith, visits a sick cottager. There are many interesting aspects to this episode. The poor, we learn, live in hovels; the visitors from the genteel world are struck by 'the wretchedness of the place', both within and without the houses. The tone of Emma's reflections on the plight of the poor indicates the massive gulf that is fixed between the professional classes and the miserable object of their charity. We have the uneasy feeling that she might as well be describing a different order of creation, as if an explorer were reporting on a primitive jungle tribe ('She understood their ways, could allow for their ignorance and their temptations, had no romantic expectations of extraordinary virtue from those for whom education had done so little'). There is no attempt to individualise the subject of Emma's attention, who remains a non-person ('it was sickness and poverty together which she had come to visit'). The most revealing thing about the episode is the conversation between the departing Emma and Harriet:

> 'These are the sights, Harriet, to do one good. How trifling they make every thing else appear! — I feel now as if I could think of nothing but these poor creatures all the rest of the day; and yet who can say how soon it may all vanish from my mind?'
> 'Very true,' said Harriet. 'Poor creatures! One can think of nothing else.'
> 'And really, I do not think the impression will soon be over,' said Emma, as she crossed the low

hedge and tottering footstep which ended the narrow, slippery path through the cottage garden, and brought them into the lane again. 'I do not think it will,' stopping to look once more at all the outward wretchedness of the place, and recall the still greater within.

'Oh! dear no,' said her companion. They walked on. The lane made a slight bend; and when that bend was passed, Mr Elton was immediately in sight; and so near as to give Emma time only to say farther,

'Ah! Harriet, here comes a very sudden trial of our stability in good thoughts. Well (smiling), I hope it may be allowed that if compassion has produced exertion and relief to the sufferers, it has done all that is truly important. If we feel for the wretched, enough to do all we can for them, the rest is empty sympathy, only distressing to ourselves.' (Chapter 10)

Two observations on this conversation suggest themselves. One is that the sick poor cottager is being exploited by Emma and Harriet to minister to their own self-esteem and sense of benevolence; the wretches also help the two women to see their own trivial problems in due proportion. It is also made painfully clear that their sympathy has shallow roots, and that it requires only the appearance of Elton the vicar to cause them to forget their tender sentiments. Their consciences are easily put at rest, and Emma can easily rationalise their abandonment of 'good thoughts' about the poor by suggesting that it is important to avoid distressing themselves unnecessarily by giving way to 'empty sympathy'. The left-wing critic Arnold Kettle once made the disturbing suggestion that the important question posed by Emma's visit to the cottagers is not whether she recognises the existence of the poor at Highbury, 'but whether she recognises that her own position depends on their existence'.

(C) RELIGION AND SOCIETY

RELIGION is not a pervasive theme in *Emma*. The official religion of the Highbury community is Anglicanism, whose representative is Mr Elton, the vicar. Whatever evidence there is on the subject suggests that Jane Austen is not particularly impressed by the religious system of which Mr Elton is the exemplar.

The most obvious thing about Elton is that there is an astonishing gap between his personal qualities, his outlook, his social activities and his general conduct, on the one hand, and his official role as a minister of the Christian religion, on the other. There is never a hint of any kind, in fact, that Elton is a Christian, since nothing he does is motivated by Christian belief or feeling, and much of what he does is decidedly un-Christian. He treats the ministry he practises as a profession rather than a vocation. His chief activity in Highbury is to do everything possible to advance himself socially and materially. To this end, he attaches himself instinctively to the greatest heiress in the neighbourhood in the hope of a profitable marriage. He is the quintessential social climber, and in all his objectionable activities he is abetted by his insufferable wife Augusta, who is perpetually boasting about her own genteel connections, and about their social importance.

Religion then, in its official representatives, is only nominally Christian. Christianity implies unselfish service to others. The variety practised in Highbury implies self-service, snobbery, and a resentment of whatever duties the office of vicar demands. This is suggested in Augusta Elton's impatient remark about the demands made by others on the vicar's time ('He really is engaged from morning to night. There is no end of people's coming to him, on some pretence or other'). Instead of being pleased to help others, this Christian minister sees his neighbours as intruders on his social activities, which are amply shown in all their un-Christian ugliness. His wife and himself share a malicious delight in embarrassing the unfortunate Harriet at the ball ('smiles of high glee passed between him and his wife').

Jane Austen can convey much about a character and a way of seeing things in an apparently minor incident. One pivotal one is the visit of Emma and Harriet to the poor cottagers. We may have our reservations about Emma's attitude to the wretched people whom she and Harriet visit, but at least they visit them, and show a modified compassion for them in their sufferings. In this, they make a pleasant and wholesome contrast to the representative of the Established Church. Elton meets Emma and Harriet on their way from the cottage. His remarks tell us a great deal about the practical value of established religion in Highbury:

> The wants and sufferings of the poor family, however, were the first subject on meeting. He had been going to call on them (the sick poor). His visit he would now defer.

In the light of what we know of Elton through this and other insights, Emma's remark in Chapter 19 that he is 'so good to the poor' is almost certainly to be seen as one of her many delusions. Elton is the kind of person without interest in anything outside of himself. When others have needs, he tends to become irritated ('I have nothing to do with William's wants'). It is a significant comment on Jane Austen's view of established religion that those who are paid to exemplify its teachings should be the only two characters for whom we are not permitted to feel the slightest sympathy. The Church in Highbury is seen as neglecting Christian values, and in upholding un-Christian ones with vigour and dedication.

The moral vacuum created by the Established Church in Highbury in ceasing to minister to the needs of ordinary people, especially the poor, is filled by people like Emma, George Knightley and Mr Weston, who are conscious of the moral obligations which their position as members of the ruling class demands. It is the governing class, rather than the representatives of organised religion, who set the moral tone in Highbury, which is just as well when we consider the personalities involved.

(D) PATRONAGE

PATRONAGE is a system by which people of wealth, influence and social standing offer protection, financial help, encouragement, moral support and other forms of assistance to those they consider deserving. Patronage is a significant feature of the world depicted by Jane Austen in *Emma*.

The relationship between Emma and Harriet Smith is fundamentally one of patronage, a notion that dominates Emma's attitude to Harriet, the only important character in the novel who is younger than Emma is. Harriet, indeed, is fortunate in that she enjoys the patronage of the two dominant members of Highbury society, Emma and Mr Knightley. Harriet's first patron is Emma, who is determined to improve her socially, and to see her married to the vicar Elton. At the same time, Emma is equally determined that Harriet will have nothing to do with her first love, the socially inferior Robert Martin. From this point of view, her patronage is misguided, because Robert Martin is vastly superior to Elton as a human being and as a potential husband. Her injudicious patronage of Harriet involves some significant self-discoveries for Emma. She learns the embarrassing truth about Elton's character; she also learns much about the weakness of her own judgements of people. Emma's well-intentioned patronage is, in its results, little more than foolish meddling with other people's lives.

Later in the novel, Knightley becomes Harriet's patron. His role as patron begins with an act of exquisite kindness to her at the ball, after Elton has embarrassed her by pointedly refusing to dance with her. Hitherto, Knightley has had a low opinion of Harriet. Now, finding her possessed of better qualities than he had earlier given her credit for, he extends his patronage towards her. In doing this, he partly vindicates Emma's judgement of Harriet Smith; Harriet, he admits to Emma, 'has some first rate qualities which Mrs Elton is totally without. An unpretending, singleminded, artless girl — infinitely to be preferred by any man of sense and taste to such a woman as Mrs Elton. I found Harriet more conversable than I expected'. Knightley's motives in patronising Harriet are free from any taint of self-interest. His main purpose is to rectify Emma's blunder in severing Harriet's relationship with Robert Martin; he tries, quietly and discreetly, to repair the broken relationship between the two young people. Unfortunately, Knightley's kindly patronage is misinterpreted by Harriet, who thinks that he means to propose marriage to her. The revelation of this inspires Emma's major act of self-discovery: that she loves Knightley and that he must marry nobody but herself.

Two of the other central characters in the novel, Jane Fairfax and Frank Churchill, are also objects of patronage. Jane's parents die when she is still an infant, and she is taken care of by her grandmother and aunt. It looks as if she is destined to grow up with only a limited education, and 'with no advantages of connection or improvement' on what nature has given her. An act of patronage changes her destiny. Her late father's friend Colonel Campbell takes her into his home and assumes responsibility for her education. The outcome is fortunate. She knows nothing but kindness from the Campbells, is given an excellent education, enjoying 'every advantage of discipline and culture'. Unfortunately for Jane, the patronage of the Campbells comes to an end before she is twenty, and she must return to her Bates relatives at Highbury.

It is at this point that Emma has the opportunity of extending much-needed patronage to Jane, if only to compensate for her own ill-judged efforts to patronise Harriet Smith. As the object of Emma's patronage, Jane would be infinitely preferable to Harriet. The latter has little to recommend her apart from a superficial attractiveness of appearance and manner. Jane, on the other hand, is cultivated, elegant and accomplished, a suitable and equal companion for Emma in everything but wealth. It is one of the weaknesses of Emma's character that inhibits her from extending her legitimate patronage to Jane. She nourishes an envious dislike of the only woman in Highbury whom she could befriend and encourage to their mutual benefit. Knightley, as usual, gets to the heart of the matter. Jane is disliked by Emma because the latter sees in her 'the really accomplished young woman, which she wanted to be thought herself', (Chapter 20) .

Jane, however, does attract an eager patron, one she could well do without, the vulgar and insensitive Mrs Elton. Unlike the Campbells, Mrs Elton is not an altruistic patron. She tries to take over Jane's affairs to gratify her own desire to appear significant and influential. Her patronage is neither discreet nor diplomatic; it must be advertised to the world in the most emphatic terms ('My resolution is taken as to noticing Jane Fairfax ... My acquaintance is so very extensive, that I have little doubt of hearing of something to suit her shortly ... indeed, we must begin enquiring directly'). Jane, the unwilling victim of this embarrassing attention, does all she can to repel it. It is one of the many ironies of the novel that by the time Emma has arrived at a balanced judgement of Jane's character, and is ready to patronise her, patronage is no longer necessary.

Frank Churchill's career is parallel to Jane's. From an early age, he, too, has been brought up and educated by generous patrons outside the immediate family. Born a Weston, he is given up 'to the care and wealth of the Churchills' and has 'only his own comfort to seek and his own situation to improve'. In Frank's case, however, patronage does appear to have been a mixed blessing. The over-indulgence of his patrons seems to have made him irresponsible and somewhat uncaring.

Throughout the novel, it is made clear that patronage is an essential element in the social order of Highbury. In one of the key passages of the book, Emma gives an inadequate version of patronage when she tries to make Harriet Smith abandon her interest in Robert Martin, who is a yeoman farmer:

> "The yeomanry are precisely the order of people with whom I feel I can have nothing to do. A degree or two lower, and a creditable appearance might interest me; I might hope to be useful to their

families in some way or other. But a farmer can need none of my help, and is therefore in one sense as much above my notice as in every other he is below it.' (Chapter 4)

For Emma, patronage depends on social status. She might patronise somebody lower on the social scale than a yeoman farmer, but the latter, being financially independent, does not need her help, and is therefore 'above her notice' for that reason. He is, of course, 'below her notice' in every other respect, since he occupies a lower position on the social scale than she does. There are better models of patronage than Emma's. Mr Knightley, for example, bases his acts of patronage on *moral* rather than on social considerations. Whatever he does is inspired by unselfishness and consideration for the real needs of those he patronises. Examples are his giving his last apples to Miss Bates, his rescue of Harriet from embarrassment at the ball, the help he gave Robert Martin, and his gentleman-like treatment of the difficult Mr Woodhouse.

(E) SNOBBERY

THIS is a recurring theme in *Emma* and one of the few topics on which it is difficult to see precisely where Jane Austen stands, since she offers contradictory insights of apparently equal validity. Before discussing the significance of snobbery in the novel, it is necessary to explain what one understands by the term, since it is used in a variety of senses from time to time. To be useful, a definition of snobbery needs to encompass some of the following elements. A snob is one whose ideas and conduct are marked by vulgar admiration for wealth or social position. The true snob blatantly imitates, fawningly admires, or vulgarly seeks association with those he regards as his superiors, having an exaggerated respect for rank. He also tends to rebuff the advances of those he regards as his inferiors, and to despise people he deems as having less developed tastes and attainments than he has. Being convinced of his own superiority, he is naturally inclined to social exclusiveness. In the light of such a definition, the Highbury society depicted in *Emma,* with its rigid and well-understood system of social gradations, can scarcely fail to induce a widespread tendency to snobbery. The interesting question arising from the topic is not the pervasiveness of snobbery in the novel but the way in which it is handled by Jane Austen.

The earliest major instance of snobbery is found in Emma's dealings with Harriet Smith in relation to Robert Martin. It is snobbery which motivates Emma in persuading Harriet to reject her worthy young suitor. Robert Martin is morally and intellectually superior to many of the genteel characters in the novel, and writes Harriet a letter 'which would not have disgraced a gentleman', but Emma damns him because he belongs to the wrong social class. Emma tells Harriet of the appalling social consequences to her of marriage to Robert Martin. She would have severed her connections for good with genteel society; Emma herself would have been obliged to give her up, since there would be no possibility of social relationships between a great heiress to landed property and a farmer. The true contempt of the snob for those she considers inferior to herself emerges in Emma's vision of Harriet, married to Robert Martin, 'confined to the society of the illiterate and vulgar' all her life.

The absurdity of Emma's snobbery is exposed by the wise and rational Mr Knightley, who wonders how she can think it a degradation for the illegitimate Harriet to marry 'a respectable, intelligent gentleman-farmer', whose manners have 'sense, sincerity and good humour' to recommend them, and whose mind 'has more true gentility than Harriet Smith could understand'. Knightley talks excellent sense here, and is the quiet agent of the eventual marriage of Harriet to Robert Martin. His dismissal of Emma's snobbery appears to enjoy the approval of Jane Austen. Later, however, it comes as a major surprise when Knightley, whom we are to regard as embodying the wisdom and common-sense of the novel, comments as follows on Robert Martin. His remark suggests that he, like Emma, is fundamentally a snob:

> 'His situation is an evil, but you must consider it as what satisfies your friend .... As far as the man is concerned, you could not wish your friend in better hands. His rank in society I would alter if I could ...' (Chapter 54)

Even if the context allows us to find a touch of playfulness in this comment, the fundamental point remains. In Knightley's view of things, there are people whose situations (social positions) are unfortunate and inferior to his own. More surprising, however, is the author's comment on the parentage of Harriet Smith, which appears to contradict some of the better insights on such matters throughout the novel, and which, to say the least, proposes some morally dubious notions about the relative value and significance of human beings:

> Harriet's parentage became known. She proved to be the daughter of a tradesman, rich enough to afford her the comfortable maintenance which had ever been hers, and decent enough to have always wished for concealment. — Such was the blood of gentility which Emma had formerly been so ready to vouch for! — It was likely to be as untainted, perhaps, as the blood of many a gentleman: but what a connexion had she been preparing for Mr Knightley — or for the Churchills — or even for Mr Elton! — The stain of illegitimacy, unbleached by nobility or wealth, would have been a stain indeed. (Chapter 55)

In all of this, we are faced with a paradox. Jane Austen makes us see the injustice of Emma's initially snobbish view of Robert Martin and treats this snobbery ironically. We naturally assume that the point of view of the novel is that the worth of individuals has to do not with social position or with birth, but with qualities of character and achievement. These valuable insights are compromised in the judgements quoted above.

Even Knightley, the exemplary norm of the novel, will not allow Robert Martin's outstanding qualities of character to counterbalance his social disadvantages, and therefore accords him an inferior placing in the ranks of humanity.

The many absurdities of snobbery are nowhere better captured and ridiculed than in the presentation of the Eltons. Elton the vicar is a snob in the fullest sense of the term. His snobbery is, appropriately, well diagnosed by another snob, Emma. Only one snob can fully recognise, and feel due contempt for, the snobbery of another. After Elton has dismissed Harriet Smith as being beneath his notice, and made it clear to Emma that he thinks himself a suitable marriage partner for herself, Emma provides an excellent description of snobbery in its double aspect, contempt for those deemed inferior, and admiration for those of a higher station. Emma is horrified that a man like Elton, connected with trade, should suppose himself 'her equal in connection or mind' and look down upon Harriet as his social inferior. Her complaint against Elton is that he is not a perceptive snob, since he understands so well 'the gradations of rank below him' but is blind to 'what rose above' him in the form of Emma.

'How well they suit one another!' says Frank Churchill of Elton and his wife Augusta. The latter is an outstanding snob, and her snobbery is mercilessly, though often subtly, exposed. Consider her attempts to patronise Jane Fairfax, which are a vulgar caricature of Emma's patronage of Harriet Smith. Emma, we remember, believes that the ideal candidate for one's patronage is somebody one or two degrees lower on the social scale than a yeoman! Mrs Elton's interest in Jane Fairfax is similarly patronising in the worst sense and informed by snobbery. Here is her comment on Jane:

> 'I am a great advocate for timidity — and I am sure one does not often meet with it — But in those who are at all inferior, it is extremely prepossessing.'

Here, of course, 'inferior' means 'inferior to Mrs Elton', and by extension, 'inferior to Emma', since Mrs Elton insists on seeing herself as Emma's social equal ('You and I need not be afraid. If we set the example, many will follow it as far as they can; though all have not our situations'). Emma finds it mortifying that Mrs Elton should imagine that she is on a footing with so great an heiress as herself. Mrs Elton's snobbery, however, is not to be controlled. Like her husband she looks on those of inferior social standing with contempt, and vastly admires those of lofty estate. She boasts of her brother-in-law's splendid residence at Maple Grove, and betrays a snobbish admiration for this man's standing ('we do not at all affect to equal my brother (i.e. brother-in-law), Mr Suckling, in income'). In Mrs Elton's case, at any rate, snobbery is exposed to ironic contemplation. Some of the irony of course is at Emma's expense, since Mrs Elton is merely a vulgar examplar of Emma's less considered attitudes to class and status.

(F) SOME ILLUSTRATIONS OF SOCIAL ATTITUDES IN *EMMA*

A variety of social attitudes is illustrated in the following extracts from the novel. Most of the extracts reveal the preoccupation with class, rank, and social standing which is so marked a feature of Jane Austen's world.

1 *Emma's social standing.* 'Highbury .... afforded her no equals. The Woodhouses were first in consequence there. All looked up to them.' (Chapter 1)
2 *The Churchills as snobs.* 'Captain Weston was a general favourite; and when the chances of his military life had introduced him to Miss Churchill, of a great Yorkshire family, and Miss Churchill fell in love with him, nobody was surprised except her brother and his wife, who had never seen him, and who were full of pride and importance, which the connection would offend.' (Chapter 2)

3 *Emma's prejudice against Robert Martin.* 'He is very plain, remarkably plain, but that is nothing, compared with his entire want of gentility ... I had no idea that he could be so very clownish, so totally without air. I had imagined him, I confess, a degree or two nearer gentility.' (Chapter 4)

4 *The social consequences of an unequal marriage: Harriet has decided to refuse Robert Martin.* Emma is the speaker. 'Dear Harriet. I give myself joy of this. It would have grieved me to lose your acquaintance, which must have been the consequence of your marrying Mr Martin ... You would have thrown yourself out of all good society.' (Chapter 7)

5 *The importance of money.* Emma is the speaker. 'A single woman, with a very narrow income, must be a ridiculous, disagreeable old maid! the proper sport of boys and girls; but a single woman, of good fortune, is always respectable.' (Chapter 10)

6 *Elton's snobbery. He is offended when Emma thinks he might marry Harriet.* 'Everybody has their level; but as for myself I am not, I think, quite so much at a loss.' (Chapter 15)

7 *Emma's snobbery. She has the same contempt for Elton's social standing as he has for Harriet's.* 'The Eltons were nobody ... and the Woodhouses had long held a high place in the consideration of the neighbourhood which Mr Elton had first entered not two years ago, to make his way as he could, without any alliances but in trade.' (Chapter 16)

8 *One snob, Emma, dismisses the pretensions of another snob, Augusta Hawkins (Elton).* 'What she was must be uncertain; but *who* she was, might be found out ... She brought no name, no blood, no alliance. Miss Hawkins was the youngest of the two daughters of a Bristol-merchant, of course, he must be called; but, as the whole of the profits of his mercantile life appeared so very moderate, it was not unfair to guess the dignity of his line of trade had been very moderate also.' (Chapter 22)

9 *People who have still not arrived socially.* The Coles had been settled some years in Highbury, and were very good sort of people — friendly, liberal, and unpretending; but on

the other hand, they were of low origin, in trade, and only moderately genteel. (Chapter 25)

10 *Mrs Elton has tried to patronise Emma by offering to introduce her to a useful friend.* It was as much as Emma could bear, without being impolite. The idea of being indebted to Mrs Elton for what was called an *introduction* — of her going into public under the auspices of a friend of Mrs Elton's, probably some vulgar, dashing widow, who with the help of a boarder, just made a shift to live! – The dignity of Miss Woodhouse, of Hartfield, was sunk indeed! (Chapter 32)

11 *The social pretensions of an upstart, in this case Mrs Churchill. Mr Weston speaks.* 'But her pride is arrogance and insolence! and what inclines one less to bear, she has no fair pretence of family or blood. She was nobody when he married her, barely the daughter of a gentleman; but ever since her being turned into a Churchill, she has out-Churchill'd them all in high and mighty claims; but in herself, I assure you, she is an upstart.' (Chapter 36)

12 *An upstart, Mrs Elton, has a horror of upstarts.* 'Maple Grove has given me a thorough disgust to people of that sort; for there is a family in that neighbourhood who are such an annoyance to my brother and sister from the airs they give themselves! Your description of Mrs Churchill made me think of them directly. People of the name of Tupman, very lately settled there, and encumbered with many low connections but giving themselves immense airs, and expecting to be on a footing with the old established families.' (Chapter 36)

13 *The importance of being long established, of coming from the right place, and of making one's money respectably. Again, the Tupmans are in question.* 'A year and a half is the utmost they can have lived at West Hall; and how they got their fortune nobody knows. They came from Birmingham, which is not a place to promise much, you know, Mr Weston. One has not great hopes from Birmingham. I always say there is something direful in the sound.' (Chapter 36)

14 *Emma's horror at the idea that Mr Knightley might marry Harriet Smith.* Mr Knightley and Harriet Smith! Such an elevation on her side! Such a debasement on his! It was horrible to Emma to think how it must sink him in the general opinion, to foresee the smiles, the sneers, the merriment it would prompt at his expense; the mortification and disdain of his brother ... How Harriet could ever have had the presumption to raise her thoughts to Mr Knightley! (Chapter 47)

15 *Harriet's marriage to Robert Martin changes the nature of her relationship with Emma. Social barriers are now erected.* Harriet, necessarily drawn away by her engagements with the Martins, was less and less at Hartfield; which was not to be regretted. The intimacy between her and Emma must sink; their friendship must change into a calmer sort of goodwill; and fortunately, what ought to be, and must be, seemed already beginning, and in the most gradual, natural manner. (Chapter 55)

Some Themes of the Novel

(A) MARRIAGE AND MATCH-MAKING

THE dominant theme of *Emma* is marriage. All the important activities of the novel are focused on various attempts to arrange marriages or even to hinder or prevent them. The entire narrative is framed by weddings. The novel begins on the wedding-day of Miss Taylor to Mr Weston. It develops a new impetus and direction with the arrival at Highbury of the new bride Mrs Elton in Chapter 22, and ends with the matches of the three central couples: Knightley and Emma, Robert Martin and Harriet, and Frank Churchill and Jane Fairfax. Most of what happens in between has to do with people proposing and being accepted or rejected, marriage plans projected and falling through, and various well-meant attempts at match-making.

The importance of marriage as a theme in *Emma* has to be judged against the background of ideas on the subject in Jane Austen's day. For middle-class women such as Emma and Jane Fairfax, making a suitable marriage was an important matter, having a greater urgency in Jane's case than in Emma's. The latter's great wealth makes her independent of the need to marry. There is an interesting and amusing exchange between Emma and Harriet in Chapter 10 on the subject of marriage. Emma declares that she has 'none of the usual inducements of women to marry'. Apart from love, which is the only thing that would induce her to marry, she mentions three reasons why a middle-class woman might be anxious to change her single state: to increase her material prosperity ('fortune'); to increase her social importance ('consequence') and to have an occupation ('employment') as mistress of a house.

Since Emma already has vast wealth, as much social consequence as any husband could give her, and adequate employment and authority in her father's house at Hartfield, she does not see marriage as a pressing issue, and a loveless marriage would, for her, be absurd in the circumstances. She can understand why some women might think differently, particularly when their financial situation differed from hers. As she says to Harriet, 'A single woman, with a very narrow income, must be a ridiculous, disagreeable, old maid!' On the other hand, a single woman with a good fortune, like herself, is considered respectable by society, and is not obliged to bear a social stigma. Emma, then, even if she were to remain a spinster, would be a fortunate one. The perfect model of the unfortunate spinster is Jane Fairfax's aunt, Miss Bates, whose good nature and benevolence cannot compensate, in Emma's eyes at any rate, for her straitened financial circumstances. Emma finds her 'too good-natured and too silly', but admits she is to the taste of everybody else, 'though single and though poor'.

The most interesting character who is both single and poor is Jane Fairfax. She herself sees this combination of circumstances as posing major problems for her. As a single woman of respectable family, Jane can choose between marriage, remaining an impoverished spinster, and pursuing the career designated for her by Mrs Elton, that of governess. Jane herself is only too conscious of miseries attendant on this career. She thinks of it as involving the sale of human intellect. Offices where posts as governess are arranged Jane sees as little better than slave-trading posts. Her comment to Mrs Elton on these matters is one of the most impressive pieces of social criticism in the novel:

> 'I did not mean, I was not thinking of the slave-trade', replied Jane: 'governess-trade, I assure you, was all that I had in view; widely different certainly as to the guilt of those who carry it on; but as to the greater misery of the victims, I do not know where it lies.'

Fortunately for Jane, she escapes this hideous fate by marrying Frank Churchill.

THE REQUIREMENTS FOR MARRIAGE

In the world of *Emma,* marriage depends a great deal on two fundamental factors: equality of social class and background, and equality of fortune. It is true that Jane Austen does not allow these two considerations to dominate to the exclusion of all others. Jane Fairfax, for example, although she has no personal fortune, nevertheless marries Frank Churchill, the heir to a great property. But in the end, social compatibility is allowed to count. In spite of Emma's efforts, Harriet Smith does not marry outside her social sphere. Jane Fairfax, in spite of her lack of fortune, is in every other way Frank Churchill's equal, particularly in birth and breeding. The marriage of Emma and Mr Knightley is the perfect union from Jane Austen's point of view, founded as it is on social, material and moral equality.

THE ART OF MATCH-MAKING

Various efforts at match-making, some successful and others not, give unity and interest to the novel, and are the source of many of its most satisfying ironies. The subject of match-making is introduced in the opening chapter in relation to the marriage of Miss Taylor to Mr Weston. Of this marriage we are told that 'Emma had always wished and promoted the match'. The chapter is dominated by an exchange of views on match-making, with Emma determined to continue her activities in the field, following her success with Miss Taylor ('It is the greatest amusement in the world').

Knightley shrewdly observes that Emma is more likely to have done harm to herself than good to the Westons, by match-making for them. There is a nice irony in what immediately follows, as Emma declares her resolution to look about for a wife for Elton the vicar. In this activity, she will do even more harm to herself than even Knightley could foresee. Her attempt to make a match between Harriet and Elton ends in embarrassment for herself and for Harriet. This, however, does not end her match-making efforts. She goes on to project a marriage between Harriet and Frank Churchill. Mrs Weston thinks of arranging a marriage between Jane Fairfax and Mr Knightley, and the two Westons project a marriage between Emma and Frank Churchill.

(B) DECEPTIVE IMAGINATION AND SELF-DECEPTION

ONE of Jane Austen's favourite poets was William Cowper. In Chapter 41 of *Emma,* Knightley quotes a line from one of Cowper's poems *The Task* (1782). Cowper, gazing into his fire at twilight, was able to create images which took on the appearance of reality and truth ('Myself creating what I saw'). This latter phrase might have been chosen by Jane Austen as the epigraph for her novel, since one of the great themes of *Emma* is the capacity of the characters for self-deception. This, of course, applies particularly to Emma, since most of her problems are caused by her inability to subject her imagination to her reason. In keeping with this notion, Jane Austen coined a word for her heroine, calling her an 'imaginist'. The key passage is in Chapter 39. Harriet Smith has been assailed by a group of gipsies, and is rescued by Frank Churchill. Emma's fertile imagination takes fire at this, and cannot resist finding richly romantic implications in the fortunate rescue.

> Such an adventure as this, — a fine young man and a lovely young woman thrown together in such a way, could hardly fail of suggesting certain ideas to the coldest heart and the steadiest brain. So Emma thought, at least. Could a linguist, could a grammarian, could even a mathematician, have seen what she did, have witnessed their appearance together, and heard their history of it,

without feeling that circumstances had been at work to make them peculiarly interesting to each other? — How much more must an imaginist, like herself, be on fire with speculation and foresight! — especially with such a ground-work of anticipation as her mind had already made.

This is only one of many references to Emma's tendency to take her own imaginative speculations for objective truth. It is this that constantly leads her into pitfalls and misconceptions. Emma's first major error is in relation to Elton and Harriet. Her imagination leads her to believe Elton in love with Harriet, and to exaggerate the attractions of the latter. Her perception of these people, and of the world in general, is so clouded by her imagination that she cannot see things as they are: what she sees instead are mirages and distortions of reality, purely subjective visions. She also has a misplaced faith in her own powers of deduction, which are extremely poor and lead to all sorts of preposterous conclusions. She has an astonishing facility for manufacturing a whole series of 'realities' which have no foundation in objective fact, and for ignoring evidence which is clear to everybody else. For example, she has no doubt that Mr Elton is falling in love with Harriet. 'You are his object', she tells the latter, 'and you will soon receive the completest proof of it!' She also sees Mr Knightley falling in love with Harriet ('Mr Knightley and Harriet Smith! — It was an union to distance every wonder of the kind') and Frank Churchill falling in love with Harriet after the rescue from the gipsies.

These are all fantasies. What Emma does not see is that Elton is pursuing herself, and not Harriet, and that Frank Churchill and Jane Fairfax are engaged in deep deception about their own relationship. She cannot even see the true nature of what most concerns herself: the relationship between her and Mr Knightley. There is an amusing, ironic encounter between Emma and Knightley on the subject of Frank Churchill and Jane Fairfax. The dialogue comes to the heart of the contrast between Emma and Knightley where imagination and reality are concerned. Knightley, unlike Emma, has a mind firmly anchored in realities; he is not subject to fantasies or delusions. He has been observing Frank Churchill and Jane Fairfax closely, and has come to the conclusion, based on firm evidence, that there is a greater degree of intimacy between them than they are prepared to admit to the world at large. Emma, on the other hand, will not see things this way. The irony of the following exchange between Emma and Knightley lies in the fact that Emma, the wild imaginist, accuses Knightley, the realist, of giving way to imaginative flights:

> 'My dear Emma', said he at last, with earnest kindness, 'do you think you perfectly understand the degree of acquaintance between the gentleman and lady we have been speaking of?'
> 'Between Mr Frank Churchill and Miss Fairfax? Oh yes, perfectly — why do you make a doubt of it?'
> 'Have you never at any time had reason to think that he admired her, or that she admired him?'
> 'Never, never!' — she cried with a most open eagerness — 'Never, for the twentieth part of a moment, did such an idea occur to me. And how could it possibly come into your head?'
> 'I have lately imagined that I saw symptoms of attachment between them — certain expressive looks, which I did not believe meant to be public.'
> 'Oh, you amuse me excessively. I am delighted to find that you can vouchsafe to let your imagination wander .... (Chapter 41)

Emma's illusion has been that Frank Churchill is in love with her. In this, her imagination misleads her, and her vanity is flattered. Emma also misreads the signs in relation to Jane Fairfax. She creates a fantasy relationship between Jane and Dixon, no doubt inspired by her resentment of Jane, who is 'so idolised and so cried up'. In this case, Emma's imagination powerfully ministers to her own self-esteem. To believe that Jane Fairfax is disreputable in some way or other is to feel superior to her. She fondly, and baselessly, imagines Jane to be guilty of 'having seduced Mr Dixon's affections from his wife' (Chapter 20). This gives her a comforting sense of moral superiority.

Emma's imagination is again shown powerfully at work in the scene where she meets Frank Churchill on his return to Highbury. Frank is restless and hurries away. Emma interprets Frank's hasty departure as a sign that he is now less in love with her than he was, but she insists on believing that her power over his feelings is still very strong, and that he must hurry away to avoid being once again captivated by her:

> She had no doubt as to his being less in love — but neither his agitated spirits, nor his hurrying away, seemed like a perfect cure; and she was rather inclined to think it implied a dread of her returning power, and a discreet resolution of not trusting himself with her long. (Chapter 37)

Emma's imagination is playing her totally false here. Frank's 'agitated spirits' have absolutely nothing to do with Emma, and he is hurrying away not to escape from her charms, but to see Jane Fairfax. In fact, Emma's imagination is twice deceived in relation to Frank. She has already been making plans for Frank and Harriet to become lovers. In Chapter 31 we learn that she intends to discourage Frank's 'love' for herself, but to encourage the notion that her 'beautiful little friend' Harriet should take her place. A flattering comment of Frank's about Harriet is enough to inspire this fantasy ('His recollection of Harriet, and the words which clothed it, ... suggested to her the idea of Harriet's succeeding her in his affections. Was it impossible? — No'). Her imagination also deceives her in making her think that Harriet is attracted to Frank.

In fairness to Emma, it must be said that the repeated blunders into which her imagination leads her are ultimately the means of bringing about self-recognition and self-awareness. She is utterly humiliated when her protegée Harriet seems to her to be about to marry Knightley, and sheds her sense of superiority, which her active imagination has so long fed. As she recognises the need to suspend the activities of her overworked imagination, she begins to see things as they really are. As she approaches the kind of objectivity of which

Knightley is so fine an exemplar, she becomes worthy of him.

Emma, of course, is not the only character with an overactive and deceiving imagination. Most of the characters in the novel live within a world of their own creation, in which everything is interpreted in the light of their own egotistical desires. Consider Mr Woodhouse, for example. His little world is one in which people like to restrict their movements as much as possible, dread almost every kind of weather, prefer poor food to good, fear draughts and dread catching colds ('They would catch worse colds at the Crown than anywhere'), and detest change of any kind. Frank Churchill creates a world in which the prime value is the deception of others, and in which nobody else's feelings are allowed to count. Miss Bates creates a world in which her own relatives are of such all-absorbing interest that everybody is constantly longing for news of them.

The world of the Eltons is one in which superficial charm is of supreme importance, even if this conceals utter vulgarity. Harriet's private world is somewhat different from the other worlds. It is the creation not of herself but of Emma. It is a pleasant, flattering world for Harriet to inhabit, and a convenient one. All this dull girl is obliged to do is to wait for her social and intellectual superiors, Elton, Knightley and Churchill, to make her proposals of marriage. Even Knightley is made to suffer a touch of imaginative self-deception. His view of the world is distorted by his envy of Frank Churchill's apparent success as Emma's admirer. Knightley is blind to the fact that his bitter dislike of Churchill is founded on jealousy. All of these self-created worlds are autonomous. The characters of the book, living in separate and disjointed mental universes, are thus somewhat alien to each other, and do not always speak each other's language. It is little wonder that the book is riddled with so many instances of misunderstanding and misinterpretation.

(C) INTERFERENCE AND MANIPULATION

EMMA AS A MANIPULATOR

EMMA is a novel in which many of the characters spend a great deal of their time arranging and organising the lives of others, from a variety of motives, good as well as bad. The heroine is, of course, the primary manipulator of other people's lives, from the beginning to the end of the book. At the start, she is proud to declare that she has been instrumental in bringing about the marriage of Miss Taylor to Mr Weston, and she proceeds from there, her main vocation for a long time being to direct Harriet's emotional life as she thinks best for the young girl. Emma treats Harriet as if she were a puppet to be manipulated at will. Being able to direct her young friend's life in its vital aspects gives her a sense of power and control, and a fascinating occupation. All of Emma's intrigues on Harriet's behalf are carried on with the knowledge or consent of the latter. Emma shows no respect for Harriet's rights as a person or as a free agent, but uses her to gratify her own selfish whims and self-regard.

In contrast to this use of one person by another for essentially selfish reasons, consider Knightley's interference in Emma's own life. Emma sees Harriet mainly as a means to an end, a sop to her own vanity; Knightley sees Emma as an end in herself, shows genuine concern for her real welfare and, unlike Emma, does not use secretive or underhand ways in any attempts to bring about his friend's happiness. Emma's dealings with Harriet should be seen as improper interference; Knightley's dealings with Emma are properly described as enlightened helpfulness inspired by benevolence. Knightley, who exemplifies most of the moral wisdom of the book, is aware early on that Emma's interference in Harriet's life is bound to do much more harm than good. 'I think', he tells Mrs Weston, 'they will neither of them do the other any good.' It is Knightley who most acutely observes the harm that Emma is likely to do to Harriet by interfering in her most personal concerns, and to herself as a result. Harriet's ignorance is a constant source of flattering self-satisfaction to Emma, while her association with the splendours of Hartfield will only make Harriet ill-at-ease in her natural environment ('She will grow just refined enough to be uncomfortable with those among whom birth and circumstances have placed her home').

At this stage (Chapter 5), even Knightley cannot foresee the full extent of the harm Emma's interference will do, particularly to herself. By filling Harriet with an undue sense of her own importance, she will make her think that the most eligible men in Highbury would be glad to have her as a wife. This is all very well until Harriet fixes her sights on Mr Knightley, the one man Emma can love. At this point Emma recognises the true folly of interfering in the lives of others.

MR WOODHOUSE AS MANIPULATOR

Like daughter, like father. Mr Woodhouse interferes in the lives of others as Emma does, and manipulates others also, but in more subtle and insidious ways. He is a hypochondriac, subject to all sorts of imagined distresses. He likes the security of his home and the comfort offered by the constant company of his small domestic circle. He does not want his way of life disturbed or changed even in the smallest detail. This is why he disapproves of Miss Taylor's marriage ('he was very much disposed to think Miss Taylor had done as sad a thing for herself as for them, and would have been a great deal happier if she had spent all the rest of her life at Hartfield').

There is a touch of harmless eccentricity in all of this, but it has a very real effect on Emma. She has to keep up a constantly cheerful front to prevent her father from lapsing into depression of spirit. He instinctively knows how best to manipulate her to his advantage, since she will, he realises, always gratify his whims. Emma's freedom of choice and movement is severely restricted by her father's tendency to interfere. This aspect of the father-daughter relationship reaches a resolution of a kind in the final chapter of the novel, when Knightley and Emma decide to marry. The overwhelming question for both of them is: 'But Mr Woodhouse – how was Mr Woodhouse to be induced to consent?' When the subject is first broached, he assumes such an air of misery that Emma and Knightley almost despair. Emma is inclined to give up hope, and the reasons for her loss of courage show the extent to which she has permitted her father's whims and selfish attitudes to interfere with her independence and peace of mind. His subtle control over her freedom seems almost complete:

> She could not bear to see him suffering, to know him fancying himself neglected; and though her understanding almost acquiesced in the assurance of both the Mr Knightleys, that when once the event was over, his distress would be soon over too, she hesitated — she could not proceed. (Chapter 55)

In the end, Emma can marry Knightley only by submitting to her father's desire for constant company and attention: she and her husband must live with Mr Woodhouse at Hartfield.

MRS ELTON AS MANIPULATOR

The most objectionable case of interference with other people is that of Mrs Elton, who is an officious busybody. Her method is to try to force her services on people who do not really want or need them. Jane Fairfax is her principal victim in this regard, but Emma must also suffer her unwanted and insulting attentions, as when Mrs Elton patronisingly offers to introduce her to Bath society. The idea of being indebted to Mrs Elton for an introduction is more than Emma can bear. Mrs Elton is even more insistent in her attempts to interfere with Jane

Fairfax's career, making unwelcome offers of help in finding the latter a job as governess in the house of an acquaintance. Emma's comment on what Jane Fairfax has to endure as Mrs Elton's companion and guest suggests how people's lives can be made miserable by the unwelcome interference of others:

> Emma's only surprise was that Jane Fairfax should accept those attentions and tolerate Mrs Elton as she seemed to do. She heard of her walking with the Eltons, sitting with the Eltons, spending a day with the Eltons! This was astonishing! She could not have believed it possible that the taste or the pride of Miss Fairfax could endure such a society and friendship as the vicarage had to offer . . . to choose the mortification of Mrs Elton's notice and the penury of her conversation . . . (Chapter 33)

Irony in Emma

AT the root of all irony is a contrast between what is being said, implied or suggested, on the one hand, and what is actually the case, on the other. The victim of irony is unaware of the contrast between reality and appearance; in a world where irony is a presiding force, what appears to be a good thing to do is really foolish, dangerous or even ultimately fatal. There are two kinds of irony in *Emma*. One is the larger irony of situation and action, which dominates the pattern of the book, and of which Emma Woodhouse is the chief victim. She is blind to the differences between appearance and reality for much of the time, acts to bring about fortunate results but only succeeds in reaping misfortune for herself and others. Her efforts at match-making, to take the central aspect of her activities, are ironically frustrated. The second kind of irony in *Emma* is local irony, confined to individual statements and passages. In such cases, the surface meaning of the statement or passage must be rejected, and other, 'higher' meanings must be arrived at.

STRUCTURAL IRONY

The irony of situation, or structural irony, arises mainly from Emma's match-making activities and their unfortunate results. Emma has a limited or mistaken view of what she is about in these match-making activities on behalf of Harriet. The reader is permitted to feel, by degrees, that Emma's activities in this regard are mistaken, and has the privilege and the pleasure of contemplating Emma ironically. This statement must, however, be qualified. The best way to enjoy Jane Austen's use of irony is to read *Emma* for a second or even a third time. On our first reading, we tend to concentrate on the events being recorded.

We share the characters' ignorance about many things. Like them, we do not know until the very end where actions and decisions are likely to lead. As we re-read the novel, we do not have to concentrate on what happens, since we already know, so we can study patterns of irony at our leisure. We now know more than the characters do at any given time, and can understand their motives better than they do themselves. We can appreciate Jane Austen's ironies only if we have greater knowledge and understanding of the characters than they themselves have. The best way to appreciate the many ironies with which the novel confronts us is to consider some examples.

EMMA, THE OBJECT OF IRONY

The workings of the plot in relation to Emma's match-making efforts on Harriet's behalf yield some rich ironies. Emma does all she can to encourage a marriage between Elton and Harriet. In her blindness she imagines that Elton is ready to propose to Harriet. The irony of her situation lies in the result of her efforts, which is that Elton proposes to her instead. There is also a piquant irony in the fact that Emma despises Elton for proposing to someone like herself, so superior to him socially, while she cannot fully appreciate that he should feel the same about being expected to marry his social inferior, Harriet.

The ultimate irony surrounding Emma's efforts on Harriet's behalf is that the more Emma encourages her friend to aim for social advancement, the more Harriet expects in the form of a husband, until she finally settles on Knightley, the man Emma has always loved without fully realising it. It is a supreme irony that Emma's plans should have the result they have; Knightley would never have known Harriet at all but for Emma's folly in promoting her in Highbury and introducing her to genteel society. The Emma-Knightley-Harriet triangle is, of course, a figment of Emma's imagination, as we are to learn at the end. The suffering caused by the delusion is, however, very acute. Her suspicion that Knightley is falling in love with Harriet produces some episodes of local irony. Consider, for example, the scene in which Knightley is trying to tell Emma he loves her. As he is about to come to the point, Emma thinks he is going to reveal his love for Harriet, and cannot bear to have him continue:

> 'Emma, I must tell what you will not ask, though I may wish it unsaid the next moment.'
> Oh! then, don't speak it, don't speak it,' she eagerly cried. 'Take a little time, consider, do not commit yourself.'
> 'Thank you,' said he, in an accent of deep mortification, and not another syllable followed.
> (Chapter 49)

Her total misunderstanding of Knightley's feelings for her here causes Emma, at least for the moment, to avoid hearing the one thing she most wants to hear: that Knightley loves her. This scene represents an ironic reversal of an earlier one in which Emma was expecting a declaration of love when none was forthcoming; here she is expecting a declaration of love for another woman, her imagined rival, when a declaration of love for her is intended. The novels of Jane Austen have many ironic parallels and reversals of this kind.

From the beginning of the novel, Emma is contemplated ironically by Jane Austen, and the attentive reader soon learns to appreciate the subtle ironies involved in almost everything that she thinks, says, plans or does, particularly in relation to Harriet Smith. Whenever Jane Austen permits Emma to speculate on her own motives in helping Harriet, we are sure to detect some underlying ironies. The following passage is a good example of this:

> She was not struck by anything remarkably clever in Miss Smith's conversation, but she found her altogether very engaging — not inconveniently shy, not unwilling to talk — and yet so far from pushing, showing so proper and becoming a deference, seeming so pleasantly grateful for being

admitted to Hartfield, and so artlessly impressed by the appearance of every thing in so superior a style to what she had been used to, that she must have good sense and deserve encouragement. Encouragement should be given. Those soft blue eyes and all those natural graces should not be wasted on the inferior society of Highbury and its connections. The acquaintance she had already formed were unworthy of her. The friends from whom she had just parted, though very good sort of people, must be doing her harm. They were a family by the name of Martin, whom Emma well knew by character, as renting a large farm of Mr Knightley, and residing in the parish of Donwell — very creditably she believed — she knew Mr Knightley thought highly of them — but they must be coarse and unpolished, and very unfit to be the intimates of a girl who wanted only a little more knowledge and elegance to be quite perfect. *She* would notice her; she would improve her; she would detach her from her bad acquaintance, and introduce her into good society; she would inform her opinions and her manners. It would be an interesting, and certainly a very kind undertaking; highly becoming her own situation in life, her leisure, and powers. (Chapter 3)

What is interesting about this passage is that it induces us to discover an ironic contrast between what we find are her real motives for patronising Harriet and her own view of the matter. To Emma's own mind, it appears that she is encouraging Harriet for Harriet's good: hence the talk of not allowing her to be wasted on 'the inferior society of Highbury', and of improving her. But as we read the passage carefully, and in the light of what we already know of Emma's disposition to think a little too well of herself, we suspect that her real motive is a much more selfish one than she will fully admit, even to herself. She is, in fact, about to use Harriet to minister to her own self-esteem, and as a means of occupying her leisure hours. The final sentence gives a good deal away about her true, as opposed to her self-deceiving, motives.

A further passage will illustrate the value of a second or third reading of *Emma* if we wish to relish the ironies which are inseparable from almost every major set of exchanges between the characters. Emma has completed a portrait of Harriet, and it is being inspected and appraised:

> 'Miss Woodhouse has given her friend the only beauty she wanted,' — observed Mrs Weston to him — not in the least suspecting that she was addressing a lover.
>
> — 'The expression of the eye is most correct, but Miss Smith has not those eyebrows and eye-lashes. It is the fault of her face that she has them not.'
>
> 'Do you think so?' replied (Mr Elton). 'I cannot agree with you. It appears to me a most perfect resemblance in every feature. I never saw such a likeness in my life. We must allow for the effect of shade, you know.'
>
> 'You have made her too tall, Emma,' said Mr Knightley.
>
> Emma knew that she had, but would not own it, and Mr Elton warmly added, 'Oh, no! certainly not too tall; not in the least too tall. Consider, she is sitting down — which naturally presents a different — which in short gives exactly the idea — and the proportions must be preserved, you know. Proportions, fore-shortening. — Oh, no! it gives one exactly the idea of such a height as Miss Smith's. Exactly so indeed!'
>
> 'It is very pretty,' said Mr Woodhouse. 'So prettily done! Just as your drawings always are, my dear. I do not know any body who draws so well as you do. The only thing I do not thoroughly like is, that she seems to be sitting out of doors, with only a little shawl over her shoulders — and it makes one think she must catch cold.' (Chapter 6)

This is one instance where our responses to Elton's remarks on a first reading are bound to differ from those resulting from a second reading. As we read the passage without knowing what the rest of the novel has in store, we tend to assume, as Emma does, that Elton is seeking to flatter Harriet by admiring the portrait with uncritical and unalloyed enthusiasm. In other words, we are as much the victims of Jane Austen's irony as Emma is. On a second reading we are in a position to enjoy the true irony of Elton's remarks, since we know that it is Emma, not Harriet, that he is trying to impress by making his flattering comments. The ironic comedy is now seen to involve both Elton and Emma, who are at cross-purposes.

MRS ELTON, THE OBJECT OF IRONY

Mrs Elton is both one of Jane Austen's most unlikeable characters and one of her great comic creations. She, like Emma, is contemplated ironically by her creator. In her case, the irony arises from the manifest gap between her pretensions to elegance and social position on the one hand, and her mode of speech and behaviour on the other. It is clear that she thinks of herself as Emma's social equal ('If we set the example, many will follow it as far as they can'). It is also clear that she regards many other people as her social inferiors. In the following passage, we see very clearly the ironic distance between what Mrs Elton thinks she is socially and what she actually reveals herself to be out of her own mouth:

> 'And who do you think came in while we were there?'
> Emma was quite at a loss. The tone implied some old acquaintance — And how could she possibly guess?
> 'Knightley!' continued Mrs Elton; — 'Knightley himself! — Was it not lucky? — for, not being within when we called the other day, I had never seen him before; and of course, as so particular a friend of Mr E.'s I had a great curiosity. "My friend Knightley" had been so often mentioned, that I was really impatient to see him; and I must do my *caro*

sposo the justice to say that he need not be ashamed of his friend. Knightley is quite the gentleman. I like him very much. Decidedly, I think, a very gentleman-like man.'

Happily it was now time to be gone. They were off; and Emma could breathe. (Chapter 32)

In Jane Austen's novels, the style, language and tone of voice adopted by the characters is always an important clue to our interpretation of them. Genteel people, in Jane Austen's world, are expected to employ genteel modes of address. Failure to do so marks them as being less than ladylike or gentlemanlike. Here Mrs Elton, for all her pretensions to gentility, clearly betrays the fact that she has not achieved a mastery of genteel speech. A true lady would not speak of her husband as 'my *caro sposo*' or as 'Mr E' or of a mere acquaintance as 'Knightley'. Even where an intimacy existed, such expressions of it were not publicly made in polite circles. Her mode of speech would sound vulgar and unduly familiar to somebody of Emma's background. Her description of Mr Knightley as 'quite the gentleman' is patronisingly offensive coming from her, as is the suggestion that her husband need not be ashamed of being associated with Knightley. Mrs Elton is here striving to suggest the social respectability of her husband and herself. What she actually shows ironically overturns her intention: she merely gives evidence of her lack of social awareness, of her unfitness for friendship with a gentleman such as Mr Knightley.

The only response to what Mrs Elton has to say in this passage is Emma's. It expresses not only her own contempt for Mrs Elton's social impropriety, but the feelings of Jane Austen and her readers as well: 'A little upstart, vulgar being, with her Mr E and her *caro sposo,* and her resources, and all her airs of pert pretension and under-bred finery. Actually to discover that Mr Knightley is a gentleman! I doubt whether he will return the compliment and discover her to be a lady!' This time, Emma is conscious of the ironic implications of Mrs Elton's display of vulgarity. Mrs Elton has tried to impress with her ladylike pretensions but has only demonstrated that she is no lady. Subsequent readings of the novel will reveal a further irony, this time in Emma's comments on Mrs Elton. With the benefit of a second reading, we can appreciate that here Emma, without realising it, is in love with Mr Knightley, and so particularly resents Mrs Elton's crude attempts to patronise him.

The Characters of the Novel

EMMA

EMMA is the key to the novel to which she gives her name, and its single indispensable character; without her, nothing of great interest would remain, except perhaps Mrs Elton. It is Emma's outlook and activities that give the novel its shape. Everything that happens is presented through her dramatised consciousness; this consciousness is, in a sense, the novel. All that happens is what she observes or does. There are very few things that we are allowed to see that she is not, and even these are closely related to her. But while we follow the sequence of events through her eyes, we are also allowed to see that her vision of the world around her is not always an objective one; we are given enough clues to be able to see for ourselves some important truths that she misses or ignores.

The overall pattern of the story is dictated by Emma's progress from initial errors and misconceptions to eventual self-knowledge and emotional maturity. The faults of the earlier Emma are presented by Jane Austen with the utmost clarity; they are seen as being inseparable from her family situation and her upbringing. In the very first page of the novel we are made aware of the elements which will cause Emma's problems, and of the fact that she herself is not aware of these as threats to her future happiness:

> The real evils indeed of Emma's situation were the power of having rather too much her own way, and a disposition to think a little too well of herself; these were the disadvantages which threatened to alloy her many enjoyments. The danger, however, was at present so unperceived, that they did not by any means rank as misfortunes with her.

Thus, at the beginning of Chapter 1 we learn that Emma is likely to have problems springing from two features of her character: uncontrolled self-will and an exaggerated sense of her own importance. Through the course of the action these faults intensify and are aggravated by others, particularly the tendency to manipulate others and to imagine that she understands the feelings and needs of others. It takes a long time, and requires much suffering on her part, to make her acknowledge her faults and their consequences, but at last she does, in a moving confession, which arouses our sympathy and compassion:

> She was most sorrowfully indignant; ashamed of every sensation but the one revealed to her — her affection for Mr Knightley — Every other part of her mind was disgusting.
>
> With insufferable vanity she had believed herself in the secret of everybody's feelings; with unpardonable arrogance proposed to arrange everybody's destiny. She had proved to have been universally mistaken; and she had not quite done nothing — for she had done mischief. She had brought evil on Harriet, on herself, and, she too much feared, on Mr Knightley. (Chapter 47)

As well as learning about Emma's weaknesses of character at the beginning of the novel, we also learn that she has many enviable qualities: intelligence, wit, beauty, wealth, social standing, and that she enjoys the love of those in her immediate circle. The happiness to which this combination of personal assets would seem to entitle her is seriously threatened by her unwarranted interference in the lives of others. Much of this interference has a comic quality, but for all that, it threatens to produce major harm for herself and others. This obviously posed a technical problem for Jane Austen: how to maintain a continuous fund of sympathy for Emma despite the unpleasant consequences of her conduct, and despite some unendearing aspects of her character: the snobbishness, the pride, the tendency to humiliate those less fortunate than herself. The main point here is that if Emma does not remain a fundamentally sympathetic character throughout, the reader will not greatly care whether she reforms or not, and will remain indifferent to the working out of the plot, which will make the novel an artistic failure.

Jane Austen is able to maintain our sympathy for Emma by using the heroine as a reporter of her own experience throughout, not in the first, but in the third, person; when for example we read that 'she had brought evil on Harriet', we automatically translate this to a first-person mode: 'I, Emma have brought evil on Harriet'. By this method of showing so much of what happens through Emma's own consciousness of it, Jane Austen ensures that we shall give every possible credit to the heroine's point of view, and make every possible allowance for her faults and failings. Having an insider's view of Emma's mind makes the reader anxious on her behalf, irrespective of her faults or merits; it puts him almost automatically on her side.

To grasp the truth of this, all we have to do is to imagine how Emma would appear if her activities in relation to Harriet were narrated from Robert Martin's point of view. We would then hear nothing of her motives or her better qualities, but everything about the pain and humiliation she is causing to the Martins. Using Jane Fairfax as partial narrator would have something of the same effect: in Jane's narrative, Emma would appear quite intolerable, as intolerable as Mrs Elton appears in Emma's recorded experience.

HOW EMMA SUFFERS

A good deal of the narrative is devoted to Emma's misdeeds, misjudgments and misreadings of other people's characters and motives. But this is not how Jane Austen allows us to judge her, since we are given abundant evidence that Emma's faults are only one side of her character. For every major episode involving her in error or misdeed, there is a counterbalancing one to suggest her better self. Perhaps the most damaging of all her misdeeds is her cruelty to the defenceless Miss Bates on the expedition to Box Hill. Here Emma certainly reaches her lowest point in the reader's eyes. Her behaviour causes acute embarrassment, and from Knightley's point of view, is morally offensive. Those on the outing are playing a game, in which each participant has to say one very clever thing, two moderately clever things, or 'three things very dull indeed'. Emma's retort to Miss Bates is gratuitously offensive, an affront to decent human feelings:

> 'Oh! very well,' exclaimed Miss Bates; 'then I need not be uneasy. "Three things very dull indeed." That will just do for me, you know I shall be sure to say three dull things as ever I open my mouth, shan't I?' (Looking round with the most good-humoured dependence on everybody's assent) 'Do not you all think I shall?'
> Emma could not resist.
> 'Ah! ma'am, but there may be difficulty. Pardon me — but you will be limited as to number — only three at once.'
> Miss Bates, deceived by the mock ceremony of her manner, did not immediately catch her meaning; but when it burst upon her, it could not anger, though a slight blush showed that it could pain her.
> 'Ah! — well — to be sure. Yes, I see what she means' (turning to Mr Knightley), 'and I will try to hold my tongue. I must make myself very disagreeable, or she would not have said such a thing to an old friend.' (Chapter 43)

Knightley shows Emma the full iniquity of what she does here. As he points out to her later, it is unpardonable to expose the harmless woman to ridicule in the presence of people who might be guided by Emma's treatment of her. Knightley's words are seen to have their effect; Emma feels 'anger against herself, mortification, deep concern'; she has never been 'so agitated, mortified, grieved, at any circumstance in her life'. It is true that some of this emotion arises from her fear that Knightley thinks ill of her, but she is genuinely grieved at having been 'so brutal, so cruel' to Miss Bates. Tears of sorrow are followed by a visit to Miss Bates the next morning, 'in the warmth of true contrition'. Jane Austen has given us a vivid account of Emma's insult to Miss Bates, but the account of Emma's remorse is even more extended, vivid and moving.

THE REPENTANT EMMA

Jane Austen, then, in order to preserve a necessary degree of sympathy for Emma, ensures that whenever she does something improper, she is shown to suffer deeply for it. In the early chapters, we see her foolishly persuading Harriet that she should like Elton. When her scheme ends in disaster, we are shown in detail how chastened and mortified she is ('Every part of it brought pain and humiliation', Chapter 16). She does all she can to drive Elton from Harriet's thoughts, 'striving to occupy and amuse her'.

Much later, when all her schemes seem to have failed, and when she believes that Harriet may be about to gain Knightley's affections, Emma reaches a clearer understanding of her own faults and limitations than she has ever had. Whatever criticism we may feel obliged to make of her foolish, irresponsible behaviour towards Harriet, the Martins, Miss Bates and Jane Fairfax, Jane Austen ensures that this is more than offset by the sympathy aroused in us by her self-criticism and mental suffering. She is seen to engage in 'unpleasant reflection' on her past conduct and to experience 'bitter regret' and a sense of 'past injustice towards Miss Fairfax'. Her suspicions that Jane had formed an improper attachment to Mr Dixon she now regards as 'abominable'.

Emma is deeply depressed as well as chastened: the prospect before her is 'threatening to a degree that could not be entirely dispelled'. At this point (Chapter 48) the reader is disposed to wish Emma well, and to hope that she will find happiness with Knightley. The bleak alternative which darkens her spirits is that she will be isolated from the human sources of her happiness, left to occupy Hartfield with her melancholic father, to cheer him 'with the spirits only of ruined happiness', deprived of the full love and attention of Mrs Weston. Whatever Emma's faults, nobody who shares her despair for the future can wish her anything but a happy resolution of her problems.

EMMA'S SELF-DECEPTION

Many readers have found the clue to Emma's character in her tendency to self-deception. There is a certain wilfulness in this; it suits her deepest purposes and instincts to deceive herself from time to time. Consider her response when Mrs Weston suggests that Knightley might marry Jane Fairfax:

> Her objections to Mr Knightley's marrying did not in the least subside. She could see nothing but evil in it. It would be a great disappointment to Mr John Knightley (Knightley's brother); consequently to Isabella. A real injury to the children — a most mortifying change, and material loss to them all; — a very great deduction from her father's daily comfort — and, as to herself, she could not at all endure the idea of Jane Fairfax at Donwell Abbey. A Mrs Knightley for them all to give way to! — No, Mr Knightley must never marry. Little Henry must remain the heir of Donwell. (Chapter 26)

Some of the reasons for not wanting Knightley married to Jane are almost childish ('a great deduction from her father's daily comfort', for example). Her final one, that Henry, John Knightley's and Isabella's son, must inherit Donwell, is later shown to be spurious, since when she herself becomes engaged to Knightley, little Henry's claims are quickly forgotten. Her fundamental, unacknowledged objection to Knightley's marrying Jane or anybody else is that she is in love with him herself.

Jane Austen described Emma as 'the heroine whom no body but myself will much like'. As we have seen, Jane Austen does a great deal to make us like Emma, for all her faults.

Many of these faults are inseparable from the values of her society. In the social world in which she is placed, it would be difficult for somebody like Emma to avoid being somewhat materialistic, complacent, superior and snobbish.

Given the circumstances of her upbringing, it is easy to see why Emma behaves like a spoilt child. In any moral judgement on her character, account must be taken of her father's generally damaging influence on her life. His negative influence works on her in two ways. His premature senility and lack of intellectual power make it impossible for him to offer any kind of intelligent or stimulating conversation; it is left mainly to Mr Knightley to provide this. The second of the disabilities from which she suffers at the hands of such a father is that he never makes her aware of her failings and has nothing to offer her in the way of constructive criticism. Indeed, whatever guidance is given at Hartfield is given by Emma herself. It is she, rather than her father, who fills the parental role. He does little or nothing to promote her welfare; she does a great deal to promote his.

The nature of the normal parent-child relationship is thus inverted at Hartfield. One of Emma's most attractive features is her solicitous, caring attitude to her most difficult and demanding father. She knows instinctively what will worry and distress him, and is constantly occupied in protecting him from even the slightest inconveniences, and in furthering his interests. She has a sense of responsibility far in excess of what people of her age (she is only twenty-one) would normally have. She also has to bear an undue weight of power and authority in the vacuum left by her helpless father. Little wonder, then, that she exerts her power, authority and benevolence well beyond the boundaries of Hartfield. Having almost unlimited power and responsibility at home, she is naturally tempted to exert these abroad.

MR KNIGHTLEY

MR KNIGHTLEY is central to the novel in a variety of ways. Even though neither he nor Emma realises this for a long time, he is the focus of her existence, and she of his. He provides the kind of moral and practical guidance that her father is unable to give her, and is an ideal confidant. In the moral scheme of the novel, he is a pivotal character, since he clearly represents the author's exemplary norm: in a world of disturbed personalities and aberrant judgements, he is a haven of rationality and sound common sense.

To estimate Knightley's moral worth, we only have to place him against the other male characters of the novel. Elton is an egotistical snob, with little regard for the fundamental decencies of social life. The contrast between him and Knightley in this respect is forced on our attention in the embarrassing episode of the Crown Ball, when Elton gleefully mortifies Harriet by refusing to dance with her and Knightley chivalrously rescues her from her distress. Frank Churchill, like Elton, is an egotist, with little regard for other people's feelings; Mr Woodhouse is a doting, ineffectual hypochondriac and another egotist. John Knightley is somewhat grim and unsocial with more than his share of egotism, while Mr Weston lacks judgement. From all these versions of inadequate and mainly unappealing human nature, George Knightley stands out as a balanced, agreeable, humane figure, considerate of others in an unobtrusive way, and free of the destructive egotism which mars so many of the other characters in the novel, both male and female.

Jane Austen's introduction of her characters is usually significant. A favourable or hostile first comment gives the key to what will follow. George Knightley is first described as 'a sensible man', and this is how he appears throughout. In a novel where so many of the characters see the world around them badly out of focus, and are misled by imagination and gross delusion, Knightley is an objective, honest observer, invariably able to put Emma right when she falls into error, and usually able to read character and motive with unerring accuracy. This talent he displays in relation to Harriet Smith, Mr and Mrs Elton, Jane Fairfax and Frank Churchill; he understands Emma and her problems better than she herself does.

Knightley's judgement of Harriet Smith is perfectly sound. Whereas Emma exaggerates the young girl's merits and possibilities, Knightley finds her commonplace and unremarkable, and an unsuitable companion for Emma ('She knows nothing herself, and looks upon Emma as knowing everything .... Her ignorance is hourly flattery'). Later, in the euphoria of his engagement to Emma, Knightley grants Harriet's good qualities: 'I am convinced of her being an artless, amiable girl, with very good notions, very serious good principles, and placing her happiness in the affections and utility of domestic life'. Much of this, he tells Emma, 'she may thank you for'.

For once, perhaps understandably, Knightley is letting his heart rule his head, since he is giving both Harriet and Emma a little more praise than they deserve. His description of Harriet is an index of his manner and personality. It reads like a character-reference from a rather pompous employer or school head, and suggests the speaker's unremitting seriousness.

KNIGHTLEY'S JEALOUSY

It would be misleading to think of Knightley as a godlike, self-sufficient authority on everything, invulnerable to doubt, fear, error or passion, and presiding in a superior, self-satisfied manner over the erring beings of Highbury, patiently correcting faults and exercising superior judgement. If he were simply a combination of all these perfections he would be nothing more than a boring abstraction. Fortunately for the reader, Jane Austen endows Knightley with appealing human qualities, with weaknesses as well as strengths. His judgement is better than anybody else's, and he is admirably tactful and restrained in his dealings with other people. He is a strong, reliable guide, friend and lover to Emma. But like every credible fictional character he is vulnerable in some respects. His vulnerability is nowhere more obvious than in his fretful responses to Frank Churchill's dealings with Emma. After he has finally assured himself of Emma's undivided love for himself, Knightley is able to acknowledge the powerful feelings he has so well concealed: 'On his side, there had been a long standing jealousy .... He had been in love with Emma, and jealous of Frank Churchill, from about the same period, one sentiment having probably enlightened him as to the other.' (Chapter 49)

Knightley's love for Emma, and his accompanying envy of Frank Churchill obviously inspire many of his unfavourable opinions of this young man's character. The fact that his unfavourable opinions of Churchill are based on intuition and personal dislike as well as jealousy does not make them any less valid. He is right in finding Churchill guilty of 'inconsideration and thoughtlessness'. There are times when Knightley is made to appear somewhat like Emma, mainly when his feelings for the latter are highly engaged. At one point his reason and judgement are clouded by his feelings, and he misreads evidence much as Emma does, although most of his conclusions are sound:

> Mr Knightley, who, for some reason best known to himself, had certainly taken an early dislike to Frank Churchill, was only growing to dislike him more. He began to suspect him of some double-dealing in his pursuit of Emma. That Emma was his object appeared indisputable. Every thing declared it; his own attentions, his father's hints, his mother-in-law's guarded silence: it was all in unison; words, conduct, discretion, and indiscretion, told the same story. But while so many were devoting him to Emma, and Emma herself making him over to Harriet, Mr Knightley began to suspect him of some inclination to trifle with Jane Fairfax. (Chapter 41)

Here, Knightley does what Emma habitually does: he allows his imagination to construct a false picture of reality based on a few random hints and indications. His conclusion that Emma is Churchill's object has no more basis in fact than Emma's conclusion that Harriet Smith is Elton's object. On the other hand, Knightley is far more perceptive than Emma is in suspecting the true nature of the Churchill-Jane Fairfax relationship.

KNIGHTLEY, THE GENTLEMAN

There can be little doubt that Knightley represents some of Jane Austen's most cherished ideals. He is a convincing representation of a civilised man of the upper-middle class, to which Jane Austen herself belonged. His ideals are noble ones and his conduct is invariably gentleman-like. He has a proper sense of his own social position and the duties this entails. Like a true gentleman, he will not meddle in other people's affairs where his interest is not welcome. He does, however, help those in distress whenever the occasion demands. He shows admirable chivalry in rescuing Harriet from her embarrassment at the Ball. Acts of kindness and generosity such as this come naturally to him. His generosity of spirit and consideration for others are shown in his sensitive response to the cruel insult offered by Emma to Miss Bates. His kindness takes a practical turn: he is instrumental in the reconciliation of Harriet Smith and Robert Martin, for example.

Apparently trivial details help establish Knightley's combination of firmness and good manners. Perhaps the best illustration of this is found in Chapter 28, which features Knightley and Mrs Bates in a lengthy comic exchange, he on horseback, she conversing with him through a window. It would take a man with the patience of Job to endure Miss Bates's chatter for any length of time. Knightley is civilised enough and self-controlled enough to be able to convey his impatience at Miss Bates's stream of trivial, inconsequential comment, while still not appearing unkind or causing her the slightest offence. His breeding and social position give him sufficient confidence to speak his mind directly and straightforwardly, when less well-bred people might think it necessary or advisable to conceal their feelings in a hypocritical show of politeness. A contrast with Emma will confirm this feature of his character. Emma, like Knightley, finds Miss Bates ridiculous, but her response, expressed in the most elegant way (Chapter 43) in the form of an unconsidered witticism, is deeply hurtful.

Knightley's consideration for the feelings of others saves him from inflicting this kind of wound on the sensibilities of Miss Bates. It is also to his credit that he feels deeply for Miss Bates following Emma's blundering insensitivity, and that he makes Emma aware of her wrongdoing ('How could you be so insolent in your wit to a woman of her character, age, and situation?'). Knightley's behaviour illustrates his central importance as Jane Austen's version of a truly civilised man, one whose conduct and outlook conform to the highest moral standards. What he professes to be, and what he does, are one and the same. We only have to contrast him in this respect with Elton to be aware of his superiority as a moral being.

KNIGHTLEY AND EMMA

Knightley's relationship with Emma is the most important one in the novel; in a sense, the whole book is about this relationship, and everything else is secondary to it. It is far from being a conventional love relationship. From the beginning, Knightley appears to Emma as more an authority-figure than a lover, a substitute for her ineffectual father. He takes on the role of teacher and moral guide, offering a continuous stream of just and necessary criticism. In all of this, she takes the role of a pupil, although this is somewhat complicated by the fact that she often defends herself against his criticisms in a lively, spirited way.

An important element in the relationship is the considerable disparity in age between the two. He is thirty-seven or thirty-eight when she is not quite twenty-one. In an interesting passage, we are made aware of some of the implications of the gap between their ages, as each of them sees it. Emma is pleased that she and Knightley think alike about their common nephews and nieces, the children of Isabella and John Knightley. Mr Knightley pursues the subject of the differences in outlook between Emma and himself:

> 'If you were as much guided by nature in your estimate of men and women, and as little under the power of fancy and whim in your dealings with them, as you are where these children are concerned, we might always think alike.'
> 'To be sure — our discordancies must always arise from my being in the wrong.'
> 'Yes,' said he, smiling — 'and reason good. I was sixteen years old when you were born.'
> 'A material difference, then,' she replied — 'and no doubt you were much my superior in judgement at that period of our lives; but does not the lapse of one-and-twenty years bring our understandings a good deal *nearer?*'
> 'Yes — a good deal nearer.'
> 'But still not near enough to give me a chance of being right, if we think differently.'
> 'I still have the advantage of you by sixteen years' experience, and by not being a pretty young woman and a spoiled child. Come, my dear Emma, let us be friends and say no more about it.'
> (Chapter 12)

Emma's claim that as time passes the difference between the two in experience and maturity of judgement will be reduced turns out to be justified by events. As the events unfold, the gap between the two gradually diminishes. As Emma learns about life through experience, error and misunderstanding, she gains the wisdom and insight appropriate to an older person. Knightley changes too, mainly under Emma's influence, but also because of the emotions aroused in him by Frank Churchill's apparent interest in Emma. As

Emma assumes the maturity of someone beyond her years, Knightley grows younger in spirit and in heart.

As the true strength of his love for Emma dawns on him, Knightley abandons some of his sober self-sufficiency and becomes youthful, excitable, somewhat unstable emotionally. In this new role, Jane Austen exposes him to faintly comic scrutiny. Here we see him in a state of emotional and intellectual confusion following his acceptance by Emma:

> He had found her agitated and low. — Frank Churchill was a villain. — He heard her declare that she had never loved him. Frank Churchill's character was not desperate. — She was his own Emma, by hand and word, when they returned into the house; and if he could have thought of Frank Churchill then, he might have deemed him a very good sort of fellow. (Chapter 49)

Emma and Knightley are, at the beginning, two self-sufficient characters. Their gradual coming together is marked by a steady erosion of self-sufficiency and a loss of independence.

JANE FAIRFAX

ALL the characters of the novel are placed in relation to the central character, Emma. Jane Fairfax is presented in a symbolic relationship with Emma, with whom she is both contrasted and compared. The similarities between the two are close. They are alike in age, social position and accomplishments. Our introduction to Jane, provided in sour and disagreeable tones by Emma, is not very promising. Harriet Smith enquires about Jane, and Emma becomes almost angry:

> 'Do you know Miss Bates's niece? That is, I know you must have seen her a hundred times — but are you acquainted?'

'Oh, yes; we are always forced to be acquainted whenever she comes to Highbury. By the by, *that* is almost enough to put one out of conceit with a niece. Heaven forbid . . . that I should ever bore people half so much about all the Knightleys together as she does about Jane Fairfax. One is sick of the very name of Jane Fairfax. Every letter from her is read forty times over: her compliments to all friends go round and round again; and if she does but send her aunt the pattern of a stomacher, or knit a pair of garters for her grandmother, one hears of nothing else for a month. I wish Jane Fairfax very well; but she bores me to death.'
(Chapter 10)

Jane is the unwilling victim of Emma's resentment. Emma's objection is not merely to the attention and comment Jane is able to attract, but to Jane herself. In Chapter 20, where Jane's arrival at Highbury is described, we understand some of the reasons for Emma's dislike. Even Emma is obliged to acknowledge Jane's beauty and charm ('very elegant, remarkably elegant, her figure particularly graceful'). Jane is a well-educated young woman of 'good understanding' and more talented musically than Emma. Jane's main problem lies in her financial circumstances. She possesses little or no material resources, and her only hope of a career, unless she marries, seems to be in what she calls the 'governess-trade', a calling little better than slavery in her eyes. In these circumstances, it might seem natural than Emma should befriend Jane, and even offer her patronage. The fact that she does not do this tells us something about both young women. For one thing, Jane repels Emma's initial attempt at friendship with reserve ('wrapt up in a cloak of politeness, she seemed determined to hazard nothing. She was disgustingly, was suspiciously reserved').

As we are to find out later, Jane is involved in an intrigue with Frank Churchill, which compels her to secrecy: hence the lack of real frankness on her part. For much of the novel, Jane remains a mystery, but this is not her only fault in Emma's eyes. She is personally superior to Emma and therefore arouses her envy and resentment. She is Emma's inferior only from the material point of view, and this makes Emma painfully aware that her own independence and social superiority are not the result of anything she has done to deserve them.

Jane, then, has an important function in revealing some of Emma's weaknesses of character. It does not take Emma long to imagine that Jane's reason for leaving the Campbells has a discreditable basis; later, she is 'willing to acquit her of having seduced Mr Dixon's affections from his wife'. Emma's real grievance is that Jane will not take part in the game she wants her to play. The relationship between the two girls involves considerable irony at Emma's expense. Jane is indeed at the heart of a mystery, but not the one Emma imagines for her. The irony goes even deeper. Emma thinks that Jane is devious and secretive, and that she herself is open and honest. In fact, as we discover, it is Emma who is the devious one, given to intrigue and the fabrication of situations, while Jane is fundamentally open and straightforward, only reluctantly involved in deception and mystery.

JANE, A CHARACTER OF PASSION

The real Jane is a far different person from the one we see through Emma's eyes. Emma's vision is of a cold, reserved, somewhat tiresome young woman. In fact, far from being cold, Jane is capable of passion and racked by strong emotion. This emerges, for example, in her bitter comments to Mrs Elton on the 'governess-trade', which excites in her the deepest feelings of resentment. She is also capable of improper conduct in her intrigue with Frank Churchill, and her choice of husband, Frank Churchill, not a particularly admirable character, casts doubt on her judgement. On the other hand, Jane Fairfax is placed by circumstances in a difficult position, and forced to make a choice between a less than ideal husband and a dismal career.

In this connection we can see in Jane Fairfax a representative of those well-educated young women whose only alternative to marriage was a post as governess. This theme is an important one in *Emma* and it is focussed particularly on Jane Fairfax. We are reminded in the strongest language of the menial nature of the governess-trade. If we find it difficult to approve of Jane's decision, we only have to make ourselves aware of what the alternative involves. What it means to be a governess is powerfully conveyed in Jane's horrifying vision of what a future in the company of the young Sucklings, Bragges and Smallridges would hold:

> 'I am not at all afraid [she says to Mrs Elton] of being long unemployed. There are places in town, offices, where enquiry would soon produce something — Offices for the sale — not quite of human flesh — but of human intellect.'
>
> 'Oh! my dear, human flesh! You quite shock me; if you mean a fling at the slave-trade I assure you Mr Suckling was always rather a friend to the abolition.'
>
> 'I did not mean, I was not thinking of the slave-trade,' replied Jane, 'governess-trade, I assure you, was all that I had in view; widely different certainly as to the guilt of those who carry it on; but as to the greater misery of the victim, I do not know where it lies ...

MR WOODHOUSE

THERE are two distinct ways of looking at Mr Woodhouse. One is to regard him as a harmless old fogey, who chatters on and on about health and sickness, draughts and colds, foul and dangerous weather. He is a comic type, the hypochondriac, so utterly absorbed by his own health that he judges every character in terms of his or her effect on it. As one might imagine, such judgements as he pronounces on others, based solely on their consideration for his own health and welfare, are not always reliable. Here is one which is reasonably so. The subject is Frank Churchill:

> 'That young man (speaking lower) is very thoughtless. Do not tell his father, but that young man is not quite the thing. He has been opening the doors very often this evening, and keeping them open very inconsiderately. He does not think of the draught. I do not mean to set you against him, but indeed he is not quite the thing!'

This sufficiently conveys Mr Woodhouse's cast of mind. His fundamental principle is that what he thinks is bad for him must be bad for everyone else and therefore banned. This kind of attitude allows for some fine comic touches, and some ludicrous and absurd ones. Consider his comment on the importance of rain in human life. In his world, small things can have major consequences and shatter the frame of things:

> 'But you must have found it very damp and dirty. I wish you may not catch cold . . . for we have had a vast deal of rain here. It rained dreadfully hard for half an hour, while we were at breakfast. I wanted them to put off the wedding.'

A SELFISH FATHER

Jane Austen's authorial comment on Mr Woodhouse is comparatively mild and lets him off lightly. He is described as 'Beloved for the friendliness of his heart and his amiable temper', but as having 'habits of gentle selfishness'. This picture of a benevolent, amiable eccentric is not true of Mr Woodhouse as we see him in action. As far as Emma is concerned, his influence is generally damaging. He is a ruthless, menacing exploiter of his unmarried daughter, and places severe restrictions on her freedom of choice and movement. It suits him to make Emma see him as a helpless child, since this will ensure that she will protect him from everything he fears and dislikes: change of any kind, risk or inconvenience. He is utterly selfish and inconsiderate of the needs of others. He cannot see, for example, that Miss Taylor's departure has left Emma at a loss and needing consolation and kindness from him. He makes no effort to raise her spirits; instead, we are pointedly told, 'he composed himself to sleep after dinner, as usual'. Again, we learn that 'he was unfit for any acquaintance, but such as would visit him on his own terms'.

Mr Woodhouse's half-alive attitude casts a shadow over Emma's life; she must fill the role of mother as well as daughter, and he subtly tries to suggest to her and to everybody else that marriage is a potential disaster. He expresses a misconceived and absurd pity for those who are married, referring to 'poor Isabella' and 'poor Miss Taylor'. Emma is vulnerable to her father's unhealthy influence because she loves him very deeply, despite all his faults. This, indeed, is one of her most appealing characteristics. She tries to fulfil his most ridiculous demands. When it comes to her marriage to Knightley, she undergoes considerable anxiety and suffering because she fears for the shattering effect it will have on her father, and is appalled at the idea of making him unhappy. Her stratagem for dealing with the problem is farcically appropriate, and involves a nice touch of irony. Up to the end, Mr Woodhouse has always used trivial means to accomplish his selfish ends. To make it possible for her to marry Knightley without antagonising her father, she, too, resorts to triviality. She is able to persuade him that if Mr Knightley lives in the house as her husband, he will have adequate protection from chicken thieves who have been active in the neighbourhood. It is, characteristically, for this ludicrous reason that Mr Woodhouse sanctions Emma's marriage.

Mr Woodhouse's character helps to explain some of Emma's main strengths and weaknesses. His feebleness of mind and his indecisiveness make it necessary for Emma to develop a decisiveness and independence of attitude, and a talent for managing the affairs of other people, however unfortunately this is directed. Mr Woodhouse is also a character in his own right. He provides much of the comedy of the novel, in company with the two other outstanding bores, Miss Bates and Mrs Elton. All three are characters who inflict boredom on others without themselves ever being boring. They are, in fact, uniformly entertaining. Their obsessive concern with a limited range of issues provides a rich vein of comedy which Jane Austen brilliantly exploits.

FRANK CHURCHILL

FRANK CHURCHILL'S family background and the circumstances of his upbringing help to account for his characteristic weaknesses. He is Mr Weston's son by his first marriage to a Miss Churchill, and has been adopted by rich, proud, arrogant and insolent relatives, an uncle and aunt. This means that Frank is brought up in affluence and with expectations of affluence. In this he resembles Emma, but he is unlike her in another respect; whereas in her case there is a strong bond of family affection, in his there is little or none, since he has no real ties with his father and has little real love for his adoptive parents. These circumstances are seen as having an adverse effect on his character and behaviour.

Churchill's main problem is his lack of personal responsibility, shown particularly in his treatment of Jane Fairfax. He secretly buys a piano for the latter, without letting her know that he is the giver, and allows Emma to speculate that it may have come from Mr Dixon, a married man. He does not seem bothered about the risk this involves to Jane's reputation. He collaborates with Emma in arranging a ball, and pays public compliments to her, at the same time commenting unfavourably on Jane and her appearance. His conduct is explained as being necessary to conceal the real nature of his relationship with Jane, to whom he is secretly engaged. This is because the proud Churchills would not countenance a marriage between Frank and a penniless young woman like Jane, whatever her attractions. To conceal the fact that he and Jane are lovers, he lets it be thought that he is falling in love with Emma. She finds his attentions enjoyable, and believes them serious. She is willing to be deceived:

> To complete every other recommendation, he had *almost* told her that he loved her. What strength, or what constancy of affection he might be subject to, was another point; but at present she could not doubt his having a decidedly warm admiration, a conscious preference of herself; and this persuasion, joined to all the rest, made her think that she must be a little in love with him . . .
> (Chapter 30)

These totally mistaken conclusions are partly the result of Emma's overheated imagination, but also partly inspired by Frank's unscrupulous encouragement.

'HIS . . . MIND FULL OF INTRIGUE'

Frank Churchill does not fully belong to the structured society to which the important characters of the novel owe their allegiance. He has no profession, and his entitlement to property depends on the decisions of a capricious old woman. He sometimes shows little respect for the social and moral codes so many of the other characters take for granted. For example, his delay in visiting his new stepmother ('mother-in-law') is interpreted by Mr Knightley, of whose view we are expected to approve, as evidence that Frank is 'proud, luxurious and selfish'. When he does arrive at Highbury, his behaviour is contrary to the decent norms of the society of that place; it is underhanded, secretive, trivial and deceptive. Little wonder that the perceptive Knightley distrusts him. Even after he writes his long letter of self-justification to Mrs Weston (Chapter 50), Knightley still has major reservations about him ('He knows he is wrong ... he is unjust, however, to his father ... Playing a most dangerous game ... regardless of little besides his own convenience ... his own mind full of intrigue').

The presentation of Frank Churchill is interesting. Most of the important characters of the novel are seen through the eyes of one or two other characters who have the most obvious interest in them. For example, we see Harriet as Emma sees her, and Jane Fairfax is mediated to us through Miss Bates. Frank Churchill, however, is seen not just in relation to one main character but to many: the Westons, Mr Knightley, Emma and Miss Bates — almost everyone, in fact, but Jane, with whom he is most closely concerned. Since Jane Austen never gives us a direct insight into his emotions or thoughts until he communicates these in his letter to Mrs Weston towards the end, he remains an enigmatic character; what he says and does can be interpreted, and is interpreted, in a variety of ways. His behaviour is sometimes wilfully wrong and is consistently deceitful. From the moral point of view he is one of the least attractive characters in the novel. His fate, however, illustrates the fact that in *Emma* Jane Austen is not concerned with strict poetic justice, rewarding good and punishing evil in strict proportion. In the end, Frank is more fortunate than he deserves to be, as the wise Mr Knightley observes to Emma:

'Frank Churchill is, indeed, the favourite of fortune. Every thing turns out for his good. He meets with a young woman at a watering-place, gains her affection, cannot even weary her by negligent treatment, — and had he and all his family sought round the world for a perfect wife for him, they could not have found her superior ... He has used every body ill — and they are all delighted to forgive him — He is a fortunate man indeed.' (Chapter 49)

MISS BATES

THREE characters shed particularly strong light on Emma's nature: Jane Fairfax, Mrs Elton and Miss Bates. It is Miss Bates who springs to Harriet's mind when she considers the possibility of an unmarried Emma in Chapter 10 ('But then, to be an old maid at last, like Miss Bates!'). Emma, of course, is perfectly satisfied that she will never become so ludicrous a figure as Miss Bates, 'so silly, so satisfied, so smiling, so prosing, so undistinguishing and fastidious, and so apt to tell everything relative to everybody about me'. Her comment on Miss Bates after the Box Hill episode (Chapter 43) is reasonably fair; 'I know there is not a better creature in the world; but you must allow that what is good and what is ridiculous are most unfortunately blended in her.' However, when Emma thinks about Miss Bates, she is much more conscious of what is ridiculous in her speech and behaviour than of her goodness of heart.

There is irony in Emma's announcement that when she reaches middle age she will not be like Miss Bates. What she does not realise is that she is most unlikely to be as universally beloved as Miss Bates is. The latter richly deserves the good opinions of those around her. She shows a disinterested love for her niece Jane Fairfax and gives her a home. She may be a bore, unlike Emma, but, also unlike Emma, she does not interfere with other people's lives for amusement. And unlike Emma, she is neither worldly nor self-satisfied. Nor does she display any of Emma's uncharitable attitudes. It would never occur to her to think an uncharitable thought or to perform an uncharitable deed. The true depth of Miss Bates's generosity, of heart and mind, is nowhere better conveyed than in her response to Emma's wounding remark about her stupidity during the Box Hill outing. Mr Knightley conveys this response to Emma:

> 'She felt your full meaning, she has talked of it since, I wish you could have heard how she talked of it — with what candour and generosity. I wish you could have heard her honouring your forbearance, in being able to pay her such attentions, as she was for ever receiving from yourself and your father, when her society must be so irksome.'
> (Chapter 43)

CONTRASTING EMMA AND MISS BATES

This tells us as much about Emma as it does about Miss Bates. Jane Austen makes use of Miss Bates in this way throughout the novel to place features of Emma's character in perspective. Consider, for example, the explicit contrast between Emma and Miss Bates. Here is how Emma is presented at the beginning:

> Emma Woodhouse, handsome, clever and rich, with a comfortable home and happy disposition seemed to unite some of the best blessings of existence; and had lived nearly twenty-one years in the world with very little to distress her.

Some of the key terms of this description are taken up two chapters later in the introduction of Miss Bates, where the emphasis is overwhelmingly on her virtues and her popularity. As we read about her admirable qualities, we are encouraged to think of the contrasts between her and Emma, who has many of the worldly advantages denied to Miss Bates but lacks her moral qualities and her capacity for inspiring universal goodwill. Miss Bates, we are told, 'enjoyed a most uncommon degree of popularity for a woman neither young, handsome, rich nor married ... and yet she was a happy woman'.

The key point of the contrast between Miss Bates and Emma is the revelation that 'she loved everybody, was interested in everybody's happiness, quick-sighted to everybody's merits'. Again, we are told that 'the simplicity and cheerfulness of her nature, her contented and graceful spirit, were a recommendation to everybody and a mine of felicity to herself'. Emma clearly lacks Miss Bates's capacity for feeling happiness and radiating it. She is not interested in everybody's happiness, but in other people as sources of amusement and objects to be manipulated.

Another central aspect of Miss Bates's character is conveyed in the same passage, where we are told that 'she was a great talker on little matters, ... full of trivial communications and harmless gossip'. It is this aspect of Miss Bates that is most memorably rendered by Jane Austen. She is one of the most entertaining bores in literature, with her steady, unstoppable stream of talk, impervious to interruption, seemingly unable to distinguish the important from the trivial, allowing one idea to borrow another, and seldom fully appreciating the significance of what she is reporting. Little wonder that sophisticated characters like Emma and Mr Knightley find her company tedious. Emma as good as tells her that it is (Chapter 43) while Knightley uses all the firmness at his command to escape from her compulsive chatter. Miss Bates's effortless command of trivial detail is finely captured in the following account of Jane's decision to accept the post of governess which she hitherto declined:

> '. . . this is such a situation as she cannot feel herself justified in declining. I was so astonished when she first told me what she had been saying to Mrs Elton, and when Mrs Elton at the same moment came congratulating me upon it! It was before tea — stay — no, it could not be before tea,

because we were just going to cards — and yet it was before tea, because I remember thinking — Oh! no, now I recollect, now I have it; something happened before tea, but not that. Mr Elton was called out of the room before tea, old John Abdy's son wanted to speak with him ... about relief from the parish; he is very well to do himself, you know, being head man at the Crown, ostler, and every thing of that sort, but still he cannot keep his father without some help; and so when Mr Elton came back, he told us what John ostler had been telling him, and then it came out about the chaise having been sent to Randall's to take Mr Frank Churchill to Richmond. That was what happened before tea. It was after tea that Jane spoke to Mrs Elton.'

MRS ELTON

LIKE Miss Bates and Jane Fairfax, Mrs Elton is offered as a parallel to Emma. Some telling comparisons between her and Emma are developed in detail. Both women are snobs. Emma has a faint contempt for the Coles, who are making an effort to overcome the social disadvantages of their association with trade; Mrs Elton looks with even stronger contempt on a family called Tupman, 'encumbered with many low connections ... and expecting to be on a footing with the old established families'. In another important respect, Mrs Elton is a parody of Emma. Like Emma, she is quite determined to arrange the lives of other people; she tries to manage Jane's affairs as Emma does Harriet's.

One of the most damaging accounts of Mrs Elton's character comes from Emma. The account is shot through with the most profound irony. According to Emma, Mrs Elton is 'a vain woman, extremely well satisfied with herself, and thinking much of her own importance, that she meant to shine and be very superior'. The irony here is that Emma, without realising it, is describing herself as well. Emma is exempt from none of the faults she finds in Mrs Elton. She too can look condescendingly on her social inferiors, and judges people by their social class.

Emma identifies another important feature of Mrs Elton's character. Her manners have been formed 'in a bad school, pert and familiar'. It is Mrs Elton's deficiencies as a social being that form the basis for some of the finest comedy in the novel. She is vulgar, affected and stupid on a grand scale, knowing no inhibitions and no restraint. She does not know her place, and is ignorant of the proper forms of dress used in civilised society. Her social lapses are constantly embarrassing to Emma and Knightley. One significant example is her breach of social etiquette in dropping the 'Mr' from George Knightley's name; this is rightly regarded as an impertinence by Emma, and is a subtle indication of inferior breeding.

Like many social bores, Mrs Elton is fond of name-dropping and boasting about her family connections. Her constant references to Maple Grove, the country seat of her brother-in-law Mr Suckling; her tiresome references to her husband as her *caro sposo;* her use of cliché ('to be quite honest'); her suggestions that her background has been affluent ('knowing what I had been accustomed to') — all of these features of her conversation mark her out as a woman to be avoided by anyone with taste and judgement. She likes talking about such exotic items as a *barouche-landau,* the name of which seems to fascinate her. She is also a supreme egotist, and like most egotists is fully convinced that nobody can hear enough about her.

Mrs Elton finds herself, and expects everybody else to find her, an inspiring topic of conversation. This is why she provides such lengthy disquisitions on her tastes, habits, outlook and background. The fact that nobody is much interested does not deter her from exposing the banality of her mind and her exaggerated self-esteem to public scrutiny. The wide gap between her estimate of herself and her actual merits and talents makes almost everything she says sound ironic. Emma speaks with justification of 'the penury' of Mrs Elton's conversation, and from what we know of her we cannot credit her with any kind of mental capacity apart from her talent for self-advertisement. There is thus an amusing irony in a declaration like the following: 'Blessed with so many resources within myself, the world was not necessary to me.'

A FIGURE OF MOCKERY

Mrs Elton is incapable of any disinterested act. She realises that patronage of the less fortunate will add to her social prestige, so she patronises Jane Fairfax. It is, however, significant that she makes sure that her act of patronage will be a matter of public knowledge. She also tries to use her patronage to place herself on a level with Emma. Note the italicised *we:*

> 'My dear Miss Woodhouse, a vast deal may be done by those who dare to act. If *we* set the example, many will follow it as far as they can; though they all have not our situations. We have carriages to fetch and convey her home, and *we* live in a style which could not make the addition of Jane Fairfax, at any time, the least inconvenient.'

One reason why Emma is repelled by Mrs Elton is that the latter is a cheaper version of herself, and caricatures her snobbery and complacency. Mrs Elton, indeed, combines some of Emma's less appealing characteristics with the outstanding social disadvantages of Miss Bates; like the latter, she is a bore and a chatterbox.

Unlike Emma and Miss Bates, however, Mrs Elton excites no sympathy but provokes a great deal of mockery. Emma's snobbery is redeemed by the elegance with which she conveys it; Mrs Elton's is further disfigured by her vulgarity and bad manners. This trait is exposed at the Crown Inn Ball. After Elton has embarrassed Harriet by refusing to dance with her, 'smiles of high glee passed between him and his wife'. The penury of Mrs Elton's conversation is delightfully conveyed in the picnic episode at Donwell. Here the garrulous, vacuous comments might well be those of Miss Bates:

> . . . strawberries, and only strawberries, could now be thought or spoken of. — 'The best fruit in England — every body's favourite — always wholesome. — These the finest beds and finest sorts. — Delightful to gather for one's self — the only way of really enjoying them. — Morning decidedly the best time — never tired — every sort good — hautboy infinitely superior — no comparison — the others hardly eatable — hautboys very scarce — Chili preferred — white wood finest flavour of all — price of strawberries in London — abundance about Bristol — Maple Grove — cultivation — beds when to be renewed — gardeners thinking exactly different — no general rule — gardeners never to be put out of their way — delicious fruit — only too rich to be eaten much of — inferior to cherries — currants more refreshing — only objection to gathering strawberries the stooping — glaring sun — tired to death — could bear it no longer — must go and sit in the shade.'

Such, for half an hour, was the conversation.

From the moral, social and intellectual points of view, Mrs Elton is seriously deficient. Like many boastful people, she advertises non-existent abilities. She is, however, a brilliant comic creation, a splendid vehicle for social comedy, who animates every scene in which she appears. The force of her personality is wonderfully conveyed: she imposes herself firmly on everybody with whom she comes into contact, and such is her lack of selfawareness and of social niceties that she cannot be discouraged in her vulgar intrusions into the lives of others. These intrusions, and the responses of others to them, provide some of the finest comic effects in the novel. Whenever Mrs Elton is present, the level of interest rises dramatically. We can forgive her all her faults for the entertainment she provides.

MR ELTON

IT is difficult to realise that Elton is a minister of religion, the vicar of Highbury. This is because we do not actually see him function in this role. Indeed, there are some hints that he finds his religious calling somewhat tedious, an obstacle to his social life and personal advancement and development. He is, for example, glad to call off a pastoral visit to some poor villagers when he discovers that Emma and Harriet have already been to see them.

Mrs Elton complains about the burdens which parish work places on her husband's shoulders, as if his religious calling were a boring diversion from his other, more pressing, interests. Aside from his apparent lack of commitment to the institutions of religion, there is also the fact that Elton seems hardly to be a Christian at all. His attitudes, speech and practices are devoid of Christian inspiration; sometimes, indeed, these are thoroughly anti-Christian. He can gleefully humiliate one of his parishioners, Harriet Smith. He is an unashamed social climber, seeking instinctively to marry to the greatest financial and social advantage. Emma's comment hits off this aspect of Elton's character: 'He only wanted to aggrandize and enrich himself, and if Miss Woodhouse of Hartfield, the heiress of thirty thousand pounds, were not quite so easily obtained as he fancied, he would soon try for Miss Somebody else with twenty, or with ten'.

Emma's words are prophetic. Elton does, indeed, try for another heiress, and gets one worth ten thousand in the person of Augusta. Frank Churchill's comment on Elton and his wife, 'How well they suit one another', is ironically appropriate and unflattering to both of them. Elton represents a less extreme form of his wife's social stances. This is why, after her arrival, he plays a relatively smaller part in the action: she has enough social ambition and self-projection for both of them.

Elton's major role is in the first quarter of the novel, where he is at the centre of a triangular relationship: he wants to marry Emma who in turn wants him to marry Harriet. Emma's early impressions of him are extremely flattering: 'I think', she tells Harriet, 'a young man might be very safely recommended to take Mr Elton as a model. Mr Elton is good-humoured, cheerful, obliging and gentle'. We also learn that he is so handsome that the girls and mistresses of Mrs Goddard's school rush to the window when he passes. Emma believes that his manners are, in one respect, superior even to Mr Knightley's, since he is more gentle, and he is said to have 'no low connections'.

Even before Emma learns something of Elton's real nature from first-hand experience, she has her reservations about him, which serve to explain why she does not fall in love with him. The passage in which these reservations are expressed throws an interesting light on Emma's own social attitudes, clearly showing that Elton, for all his attractions, is seen as not being quite up to her exacting standards. This is the key passage:

> And he was really a very pleasing young man, a young man whom any woman not fastidious might like. He was reckoned very handsome; his person much admired in general, though not by her, there being a want of elegance of feature which she could not dispense with: — but the girl who could be gratified by a Robert Martin's riding about the country to get walnuts for her, might well be conquered by Mr Elton's admiration. (Chapter 4)

The significant things here are the suggestion that a less fastidious person than Emma might look with favour on Elton, and that Elton might win the heart of a simple-minded girl like Harriet. This unenthusiastic appraisal of Elton shows why Emma cannot really take him seriously as a prospective suitor. When he actually proposes to her, she attributes this to drunkenness. She soon takes an even more damaging view of Elton. She concludes that 'the Eltons were nobody ... without any alliances but in trade' and that Mr Elton has shown remarkable presumption in thinking that a woman so superior to him as she is could possibly consider him as a possible husband. Some of her worst opinions of him are confirmed when he proposes to her in the carriage. His proposal is framed in clichés and is impertinent and vulgar ('Charming Miss Woodhouse! Allow me to interpret this interesting silence. It confesses that you have long understood me'). The vulgarity of this prepares us for the further vulgarity into which he will plunge with the arrival of his more vulgar wife. Elton is a stiff, self-important, pompous bore. He is, like his wife, an unconscious provider of social comedy, but he lacks her immense vitality and her ability to be tactless on the grand scale.

HARRIET SMITH

HARRIET is one of the least interesting characters in the novel, but she has a vital function in the general design. Her real importance in the scheme of the book is that she is exploited by Emma. The unequal relationship serves to show the folly of Emma's interference in the lives of others. This interference has unpleasant consequences not only for Emma but also for Harriet, who, towards the end of the novel, has achieved through Emma's teaching so exalted a sense of her own importance that she wants to marry Mr Knightley. The latter is quick to realise how limited a person Harriet is ('she knows nothing herself .... Her ignorance is hourly flattery'). He also sees the dangers in Emma's patronage of Harriet. Emma will be further confirmed in her sense of superiority by Harriet's inferiority, while Emma's refining influence will make Harriet ill-at-ease among her natural companions.

Jane Austen's introductory comments on Harriet provide the detached, objective view of the character against which we are to measure Emma's exaggerated enthusiasms. The objective authorial view of Harriet is coolly dismissive ('the natural daughter of somebody ... short, plump and fair ... she was not struck by any thing remarkably clever in Miss Smith's conversation'). Emma mistakenly believes that this silly, harmless girl can be 'quite perfect' with the aid of 'only a little more knowledge and elegance'. She is determined to do the very thing for Harriet that Mr Knightley thinks should not have been done. She will detach Harriet from the 'unpolished' Martins and 'improve' her. Harriet is about to become a plaything to gratify Emma's taste for arranging other people's lives. What Emma does is done not so much for Harriet's benefit as to flatter her wealthy patroness. Educating Harriet would be, she reflects, 'highly becoming her own situation in life, her leisure, and powers'.

Emma's use of the unfortunate Harriet as an instrument of her own egotism results in some richly ironic developments. Emma does everything she can to encourage a marriage between Harriet and Elton. Instead, Elton has Emma as his object, and finds Harriet socially undesirable. The profoundest irony of all involving Harriet's sponsorship by Emma comes near the end. Emma, having educated Harriet in thinking highly of herself, has to endure the shock of seeing her pupil apparently supplanting her in the affections of Mr Knightley.

Through its treatment of Harriet and her circumstances, Jane Austen's novel makes statements about English society at the end of the eighteenth century and at the beginning of the nineteenth. Harriet is not allowed to marry Elton or Mr Knightley because either of these unions would be socially inappropriate. Apart from Harriet's humble social status, there is the question of her illegitimacy. Emma had patronised her in the mistaken belief that she was of gentle birth. When the truth emerges, Emma expresses the prejudices of her time and makes us realise that marriage to a yeoman farmer is the best that such a girl as Harriet can hope for:

> Harriet's parentage became known. She proved to be the daughter of a tradesman . . . what a connection she had been preparing for Mr Knightley — or for the Churchills — or even for Mr Elton! The stain of illegitimacy, unbleached by nobility or

wealth, would have been a stain indeed .... as Emma became acquainted with Robert Martin, who was now introduced at Hartfield, she fully acknowledged in him all the appearance of sense and worth which could bid fairest for her little friend ... The intimacy between her and Emma must sink .... (Chapter 55)

For Discussion

1. We see the events of the novel through Emma's eyes; we judge them from Knightley's point of view.
2. The relationship between Emma and Mr Knightley resembles that between a wayward but intelligent pupil and a patient teacher.
3. Jane Austen spoke of Emma as a heroine 'whom no one but myself will much like'. Many of Emma's characteristics and actions are so unpleasant as to make it difficult to know why one should like her. By the end, however, she has largely redeemed herself in our eyes, as she achieves self-recognition.
4. Emma is over-imaginative, over-interfering and arrogant. Her upbringing has only enhanced her sense of superiority and certainty, and blinded her to her own deficiencies.
5. Emma is the main victim of her own errors and deficiencies.
6. The main subject of *Emma* is match-making.
7. Emma's desire to dominate everybody and everything in Highbury is the main threat to her well-being.
8. Much of the novel is dominated by self-importance, egotism and malice.
9. Money has an enormous influence on the lives and destinies of the characters in *Emma*.
10. In *Emma*, human behaviour is viewed in a comic light.
11. For much of the time, Emma's thoughts are presented ironically; we are aware of a gap between what we see as her real motives and her own view of what she is doing.
12. Mrs Elton is not to be taken seriously; we enjoy her for the comedy she provides.
13. Miss Bates is a character of great importance to Jane Austen's purposes in *Emma*. Her talk often reveals matters basic to the plot.
14. The social gradations in Highbury are presented by Jane

Austen with a rich and subtle complexity. Everybody has his or her proper place on the social scale and is ultimately forced to recognise this.

15 *Emma* illustrates the dangers of an uncontrolled imagination.

16 Mr Knightley's most attractive qualities are his honesty, benevolence, excellent judgement and common sense.

17 *Emma* is a novel about the heroine's delusions and her gradual enlightenment.

18 It is ironically fitting that Emma, who has ruled the action and so made all her own problems, should have those problems solved for her by matters in which she takes no active part at all.

19 Mr Woodhouse, like Harriet and Miss Bates, is humorous, unintelligent and largely sympathetic, a bore who is not boring, for the same reasons as they are.

20 The characters in the novel show only that part of them which Emma brings out; each character is significant mainly in relation to her.